THE ÆSTHETIC ATTITUDE

THE
ÆSTHETIC ATTITUDE

BY

HERBERT SIDNEY LANGFELD

HARVARD UNIVERSITY

KENNIKAT PRESS, INC./PORT WASHINGTON, N. Y.

PREFACE

A BOOK on æsthetics is of value in so far as it assists the reader in enriching his æsthetic experience. With this in mind I have laid particular emphasis upon a description of the nature of appreciation, for I believe that it is through such knowledge that our world of beauty is most effectively enlarged. Less attention has been given to the act of creation because a description of the special technique of the several arts, which is the chief factor in artistic production, lies beyond the scope of æsthetics. However, even though the main emphasis has been placed on appreciation, it cannot be said that the interests of the artist have been entirely neglected, for it must be remembered that it is necessary for him to appreciate before he can produce.

In maintaining the view that æsthetics should be pragmatic, that is, useful to all those who desire a deeper knowledge of beauty, I hold a position opposed to that of certain philosophers who think that æsthetics should remain entirely theoretical. Such writers generally believe that the chief characteristic of beauty is its uselessness. I have tried to show, on the contrary, that the perception of beauty is one of the most useful of man's experiences.

In order to establish the book on an empirical

basis I have attempted a description of the mental processes involved in appreciation, and this psychological treatment of æsthetics predominates, although some attention has been given to the analysis of certain art forms. The principle which underlies the psychological study is that of the motor theory of mind, namely, that to every stimulus which the organism receives from without, it makes a definite response, the nature of which depends upon both the stimulus and the past experience of the organism. That there are bodily responses to certain forms of art has been demonstrated. Although the exact nature of the responses to every form of art has not as yet been ascertained, it has seemed safe, considering the amount of data already at hand, to make certain generalizations concerning the reactions of the organism to objects of beauty.

Portions of my lectures on Æsthetics at Harvard form the nucleus of the book, which is intended for the general reader as well as for the student in æsthetics. It is not a text-book in the sense of a complete and systematic survey of all the problems of beauty, but rather a description only of those problems which I consider fundamental and which I hope will serve as an introduction to more extensive study. In a second volume I expect to cover the special fields of art and the history of æsthetic theory.

My gratitude is due to my friend and former colleague Dr. Edwin B. Holt for the inspiring talks I had with him while writing this book and for the many valuable suggestions he made after reading the manuscript. I am also indebted to Dr. A. A. Roback for reading the proof and for certain corrections in the first chapter of the manuscript, to Professor Chandler Post for his assistance in correcting the titles to the illustrations and to my successive office assistants, Miss Emma Abel and Mrs. Janet M. Clapp for their painstaking aid in preparing the manuscript.

H. S. L.

Cambridge, Massachusetts,
    March 15th, 1920.

CONTENTS

CHAPTER I

INTRODUCTION

CHAPTER II

THE SCIENCE OF BEAUTY AND UGLINESS

CHAPTER III

THE ÆSTHETIC ATTITUDE

CHAPTER IV

THE ÆSTHETIC ATTITUDE (CONTINUED)

CONTENTS

CHAPTER IX

BALANCE AND PROPORTION

CHAPTER X

ILLUSTRATIONS OF BALANCE FROM THE FINE ARTS

CHAPTER XI

THE ART IMPULSE

CHAPTER XII

CONCLUSION

THE ÆSTHETIC ATTITUDE

CHAPTER I

INTRODUCTION

§ 1. The Universal Appeal of Beauty

THE appreciation of beauty is not only an important but a fundamental reaction of the human mind. The Greek philosophers enumerated three principal values—the good, the true, and the beautiful. The first two have always been accepted. Beauty has had every position in this threefold hierarchy, depending upon the prevailing philosophy of the period, and it has also at times been banished from the world of desirable things. Yet it has continued to live in the hearts of men, even in ages which have seemed, when superficially judged, to be almost totally materialistic. Perhaps the best example of this is to be found in the late World War, when the sense of beauty provided one of the powerful motives for a free nation's participation in the struggle. It required no organized propaganda to arouse the indignation of neutrals when ancient churches, libraries, and town halls were leveled by the invaders. The indignation was immediate and almost universal, as is the case in the arousal of a primitive instinct, and it was not only because these were useful buildings, or because they were devoted to worship, but evidently and undeniably for the reason that they were works of art. Indeed, the beautiful is inseparably united to the good and the true, and the human mind that has not developed the experience of it has failed to realize the whole of reality, for the very nature of the sense of beauty is such that through it we gain a clearer concept of the other two values. The history of the race has shown that at the height of materialistic success, the desire for artistic enjoyment has been a potent factor in bringing a people back to the higher ideals which underlie a peaceful intercourse between nations.

The keen and sensitive perception of Mr. John Galsworthy has shown him the highest function of beauty. "Will there ever be more lovers of beauty in proportion to those who are indifferent to beauty? Who shall answer that question? And yet on the answer depends peace. Men may have a mint of sterling qualities—be vigorous, adventurous, brave, upright, and self-sacrificing; be preachers and teachers; keen, cool-headed, just and industrious,—but if they have not the love of beauty, they will still be making wars. Man is a fighting animal, with sense of the ridiculous enough to know that he is a fool to fight, but not sense of the sublime enough to stop him." [1]

The sense of beauty is as vital to the complete existence of the individual and of the race as is the sense of justice; it cannot be supposed that there

[1] John Galsworthy, "A Green Hill Far Away, "*Atlantic Monthly*, April, 1919, p. 527.

is any individual totally lacking in the former any more than in the latter, nor that a nascent appreciation of what is beautiful cannot be developed into a strong, useful and satisfying æsthetic reaction to the world of colors, sounds, and shapes. This reaction, on the other hand, can be as harmful as any other reaction of the organism. Its enervating influence is frequently, perhaps too often, used as an argument for its suppression. For some, indeed, artistic temperament is identified with degeneracy, and history can point to the decline of nations at the height of their artistic achievement. To enjoy beauty is often considered effeminate, and the artist, according to general opinion, is an erratic and somewhat abnormal individual.

In instances where this is true it is due to a lack of balance between the individual's intellectual and emotional states. This balance is fundamental to art, and therefore to explain its significance and the nature of the processes involved, in order that it may be more readily attained, is one of the most important aims of æsthetics. That the exposition is easier than the accomplishment is readily admitted. Nevertheless the attainment of perfect balance must be considered an ideal goal of æsthetics, as are the other factors of a perfect adjustment. Difficult as it may be to achieve, it must remain a guiding principle for the healthy development of a lasting art.

§ 2. Intellectualism versus Emotionalism

The intellectual side of appreciation has been as frequently over-emphasized as has been the emotional, which fact has led some to maintain that a study of æsthetic rules is detrimental to an æsthetic response, and that, therefore, education in appreciation is not only unnecessary but may be positively harmful. There is involved in this objection the old conflict between intellectualism and that form of intuitionalism which is predominantly emotional, and which forms the underlying principle of the romantic movement.

In the extreme form of intellectualism æsthetic appreciation is nothing more than a cold, emotionless judgment as to whether or not an object is beautiful. An example of such appreciation is that of an individual who, in viewing a certain form of architecture, recognizes that it is Colonial, or Gothic, or of some other period, and who derives his pleasure entirely from this knowledge. This is too frequently the attitude of the connoisseur. A reaction of this nature cannot strictly be considered æsthetic, although there are those whose response is little more spontaneous, yet who pride themselves upon their taste.

Intellectualism can easily be carried to excess, and when this occurs there is a break in the development of art, since very little is gained by mere rule of thumb. Whenever, as in the Classical period and in the Renaissance, rules have predominated, there has followed a reaction on the part of the Romanticists who, in emphasizing the emotional elements of artistic response, have desired, so far as possible, to abolish all formal restrictions. For them, the response must be intuitive and the result of the free play of our natural endowment.

The Romanticists are correct in their belief that appreciation as well as production should be intuitive, for the artistic response is a direct perception, with its accompanying affective states, whatever may have been the preceding intellectual preparation. Professor Croce has been an enthusiastic exponent of the theory of the intuitive nature of art, although he has been mainly interested in the abstract problem of the nature of knowledge. In his description of the intuitive character of art, he quite rightly excludes the purely intellectual judgment. He says: "The only thing that may be wanting to the artistic genius is the *reflective* consciousness, the superadded consciousness of the historian or critic, which is not essential to artistic genius." [1]

The Intellectualists, on the other hand, are correct in so far as they assert that there should be a rational background for response. While the extremes of each school should be condemned, the two positions can readily be reconciled. So-called intuitive responses can be present no matter how much there has been of previous practice and study. Only those who have not reflected upon the matter

[1] *Æsthetic*, translated by Douglas Ainslie, p. 25.

can believe that intuition in art means complete appreciation springing suddenly from nowhere. Only those who have never produced can possibly fancy that inspired creation means, to take an example from literary production, the dashing off of ideas under the dictation of the passions of the moment, without ever having had any previous wrestling with the subject. For most it is a hard grind, and even for the chosen few whose thoughts flow freely and unhampered, the result has value only if it is the issue of careful analytical study of experience in the past.

The greatest Romanticists, the men of deep and warm emotional natures, who have advocated a free rein to the passions, perhaps little realized how great and fundamental a factor of their success was the intellectualizing which preceded their final effort. Being themselves men of brains as well as of feeling, they could not appreciate what effect the doctrine they preached would have on those less happily endowed, but their sentimental disciples, usually inferior both intellectually and artistically, have seen therein what seemed to their puny minds an easy and lucrative form of creative production and have invariably seized the opportunity with enthusiasm.

The lover of emotion for emotion's sake has been enchantingly described by Professor J. L. Lowes: "Your sentimentalist, if I may risk a most unsentimental simile, is very like a penny-in-the-slot machine. Let nature drop in a sunset, or

life a heart-throb, there is a little click and a poem
drops warm and soft into your outstretched hand.
The austere requirements of clarity of imagery,
of precision and lucidity of thought, of compres-
sion and balanced harmony, of form—these trouble
the sentimentalist not a whit. All that is necessary is to reach out into an atmosphere of rosy
mist, and capture the first nebulous notion that
floats into one's grasp.

"If it is the pensive tear of a nightingale, the
absence of lachrymatory glands in that otherwise
poetic bird is beneath the notice of the divine
afflatus. The sentimentalist escapes the stern
travail of thought. The form is born in a sort
of poetic twilight sleep.

"'The greatness of an author' wrote George
Henry Lewes, in an infinitely suggestive little
book, *The Principles of Success in Literature*, ' consists in having a mind extremely irritable and at
the same time steadfastly imperial.' The artist,
in other words, must be sensitive and receptive
to impressions, alert to every stimulus from within
and from without, beyond the capacity of ordinary
men. But he must hold an imperial sway over his
impressions, selecting, clarifying, ordering, mould-
ing, filing and refiling them." [1]

We may speak of an intuitive response in any
other situation in life and the same condition holds
as in art. The expert golfer must not think of
what he should do while driving the ball or the

[1] *Convention and Revolt in Poetry*, pp. 324–326.

result will be disastrous. On the other hand, he would not be an expert if he had not given years of practice to the game. Or, to take an example from the more intellectual pursuit of chess. There are those who believe that mere practice is sufficient, that rules hamper the spontaneity of play, yet expert players assert that they spend much time in studying the plays of other men, in making thoroughly their own a countless number of different responses. At the time of playing they are, for the most part, unconscious of the results of past study and experience; they leave themselves entirely free to meet the situation as it presents itself and apparently guided by intuition, they make those brilliant moves which are termed the strokes of genius. The genius so called, however, whether in chess, in art, or in any other form of activity, achieves the more valuable results the better he has organized his past experiences and the more he is influenced by them. If we glance through the history of art, we shall find that those who have produced the most enduring works were men of great intellect as well as of deep feeling. Perhaps one of the best examples is Leonardo da Vinci, who excelled in science as well as in art. With him as with others of the immortals, we find that there was always a balance between the two sides of his nature. Great art has not been produced upon a purely emotional background, nor upon a purely intellectual one. The latter is unfortunately less often found than the former, but

given a great intellect, there can then be as much
of the emotional side as even the extreme Roman-
ticist can desire. The combination is rare, but so
is genius.[1]

It follows from the above that a definite point
of view and an intellectual background are necessary for the perception of beauty, as is the case in
any other form of perception. These should be
supplied by a study of æsthetic problems and an
application of the results to actual experience.
Many individuals visit picture galleries because
they feel it is a part of their general culture. Many
do so for the reason that they have become the
slaves of a guide-book. Together with these
motives, however, there is a certain desire to enjoy
the pictures, but such individuals have no point
of approach and derive little else than a sense of
great fatigue. Even in the case of those who do
find a certain æsthetic interest in pictures, too
frequently an ethical, religious, or historical rather
than an æsthetic, point of view predominates as
is illustrated by William James, who describes
seeing an old couple seated reverently before
Titian's Assumption, in the cold room of the
Academy at Venice. Upon approaching the couple
he heard the woman murmuring, "What self-
abnegation! How unworthy she feels of the honor
she is receiving." And James adds, "These honest

---

[1] For a discussion of rational thought and the emotions see Irving Babbitt's
Rousseau and Romanticism, especially Chapter IV and his *The New Laokoön*,
Chapter IV; also W. A. Neilson's *The Essentials of Poetry*, Chapter IV.

hearts have been kept warm all the time by a flow of spurious sentiment that would have fairly made old Titian sick." [1] It should be possible to show the difference between such an attitude and that of true æsthetic enjoyment. Obvious though it must be to most, it is often necessary to explain that such facts as that Charles the First picked up the brush of Van Dyke when it was dropped by that painter, does not add anything to the æsthetic appreciation of the portrait of the sovereign, for there is still too much of that sort of information in treatises which pretend to deal with beauty, but which actually establish attitudes toward the subject that, from the point of view of an art lover, would interfere with a true appreciation. It must be admitted that it is much easier to gain the interest of the average observer by anecdotes and descriptions which touch everyday interests, yet a knowledge of the important problems of the artist, as, for example, the difficulties in representing pictorially the three dimensions of space, or the intrinsic value of rhythm and sound in literature, will soon open up for the individual a world with which, heretofore, he was relatively unfamiliar. In other words, when we understand why the elements in a work of art are arranged in one particular way rather than another, and familiarize ourselves with the nature of the mental processes or adjustments by which such arrangements and the meaning they convey are appreci-

[1] *Principles of Psychology*, vol. 2, p. 472.

ated as æsthetic values, we shall have acquired a
background which will supply its own interests,
and an attitude which, by reason of its clear definition, can be readily assumed.

It should be the function of a treatise on æsthetics to achieve these results. That is, the value of
æsthetics should be pragmatic. The influence of
such a treatise depends upon the degree to which
the author keeps in touch with the practical interests of appreciator and producer.

It would seem as if a study of æsthetics were
more beneficial to the appreciator than to the
artist, for the latter is primarily concerned with
the technique of his art and less with the fundamental laws underlying such technique or with an
analysis of the attitude which he assumes and which
he quite rightly desires to be entirely spontaneous.
We have just seen, however, that spontaneity
may follow an introspective and analytical study,
and, furthermore, the artist is, at one stage of the
creating process, both artist and audience, just
as the audience shares, to a certain degree, the
activity of the artist. In both cases there is a very
definite adjustment of the organism to the environment, which must be thoroughly known and
differentiated from other adjustments which the
organism undergoes in the course of its development.

§ 3. The Philosophical, Psychological and Objective Aspects of Beauty

In order that the study of æsthetics should be complete, three aspects must be kept in mind: the philosophical, psychological and what, for lack of a better term, we may call the objective. It should not be understood by this that there are three distinct approaches which must, at all times, be kept definitely apart. The one involves the others, so that a constant shifting is necessary. Any attempt to keep the three methods of approach separate would appear arbitrary and artificial. In other words, this threefold division is a pure abstraction.[1]

Some authors have dealt with only one or two of these aspects. Others have misplaced the emphasis. It is therefore essential to describe them briefly and to show the relative importance of each.

Philosophy supplies the general principles underlying æsthetics in the same manner as it does the hypotheses of other sciences. It is concerned above all with the ultimate nature of beauty, and the method of obtaining this knowledge. It is further concerned with the relation of beauty to the other values of life, and with its place in human experience. For example, we shall see that

---

[1] See Münsterberg's *Principles of Art Education*, which consists of three chapters, entitled respectively, "Philosophy," "Psychology" and "Æsthetics."

one of the most important questions in art appreciation is that of the influence of ethical considerations; that is, should art exist for art's sake, or should it teach a moral; in other words, is the pleasure derived from ethical presentation as such to be called æsthetic enjoyment? Philosophy must decide whether beauty is subjective, that is merely a creation of the observer—something entirely mental, or whether it is objective, and as such an intrinsic characteristic of the object, and if the latter, whether it is entirely independent of the mind—an attribute of things which would be present even if there had never been a mind to experience it. It must also consider whether these are the only possibilities. In solving these problems, there is obtained an idea of the nature of the reality of beauty and, in the last analysis, this is necessary for the complete understanding of the æsthetic attitude. Essential as is the philosophical approach to a knowledge of beauty, it has unfortunately too often served as the only method. Many treatises upon beauty have been purely philosophical, and have left the reader with a system of vague generalities and concepts which, in many cases, remain undefined in terms of actual experience, due either to the non-empirical character of the philosopher's attitude, or because of the belief that æsthetic values from their very nature cannot be expressed otherwise. In consequence of this a certain pleasure has been derived from the clever play of philosophical ideas, but little has been offered for increasing the pleasurable reaction toward objects of art.[1]

In order to understand clearly the distinction between the psychological and the objective aspects, it is necessary for us to consider, at this point, the relation of the observer to the object appreciated, although a more complete explanation of the terms, and especially of the characteristics of that relation which is termed " æsthetic," must be postponed to a later chapter, for it is the peculiarity of that situation which will principally concern us in defining the æsthetic attitude. For the present, there will merely be described superficially the reaction of an individual to a work of art, for example, a visitor to a gallery. It is evident that as he stands before a picture, his attitude will depend upon two things—his own state of mind, and the arrangement of the pigments upon the canvas before him. This entire situation must be studied if we are to know the true nature of this relation of the observer to the picture. Psychology must analyse the behavior of the observer in so far as the peculiar adjustment called " æsthetic " is concerned; and on the objective side there must be an analysis of the arrangement and qualities of the pigments with a view to their effect upon the adjustment in question. In order to know how various colors will

---

[1] The Preface to Bosanquet's *History of Æsthetics* begins with the sentence: " Æsthetic theory is a branch of philosophy, and exists for the sake of knowledge and not as a guide to practice."

affect the eye, certain laws of color vision must be known. At the other end of the relation, the arrangement of the colors that produce the effect must also be studied. Again, we should know the possibilities of response of the human organism to lines and proportions. This can be obtained both by observation and by self-analysis or introspection. In music we have the arrangement of the sounds to produce certain rhythms; and in architecture the arrangement of the lines and spaces serve the same purpose. Our knowledge of the æsthetic value of these arrangements is not complete, however, until we know how the organism can perceive and appreciate them, nor without this psychological knowledge can we know why some rhythms are pleasing and others not. We may want to know why an organism responds differently at different times to the same rhythm, and it is again to psychology that we must turn for an explanation.

In the representation of space both in a two dimensional and three dimensional form, psychological factors of space perception are involved, and it has only been gradually through a realization of these factors that an adequate representation has been obtained. One of the most important changes in art development, that which introduced impressionism, had its source in a recognition of the mental factors in the perception of things as distinguished from the purely objective situation. Of equal importance to all representative art is the psychology of meaning, especially the manner and various forms by which the meaning can be conveyed to the mind; and in connection with this as with most of the other problems, there is necessarily an understanding of the rôle of unconscious mechanisms. Such examples can be multiplied many times. They all illustrate the general principle that any given æsthetic attitude depends both upon the mental laws and condition of the organism, and the existing objective conditions. None of these factors can be neglected. There is also a constant interaction between them— a change in mental attitude produces a change in the art object, and a change in the object through some external necessity frequently produces a change in the mental attitude.

For a knowledge of art production, as of appreciation, the psychological conditions are more important. The perceptual processes of the artist, including the rôle of memory and imagination, even the effect of fatigue and drugs, are subjects of psychological study. In fact, the ideal goal should be to determine all the characteristics peculiar both to æsthetic appreciation and to production.

In the study of the history of art, we have also the twofold analysis. Hand in hand with the investigation of the change in art forms should go that of the development of the organism, for the genetic aspect of mind cannot be neglected if we are to understand thoroughly the changes that have taken place in art. It is also, in this connection, useful to know the effects of climate and country, both upon the artist and upon the art form, for the latter as well as the former, is frequently influenced by customs and environments; for example, many of the forms of Egyptian designs are perpetual evidence of the dominant part the Nile has played in the life of the Egyptians.[1]

It is not intended at this point to give a detailed list of the psychological problems but merely a few examples to show the necessity and importance of such study. On the other hand, it should be recognized that psychological analysis does not furnish all of the data necessary, nor should the facts obtained be overestimated as has frequently been done, for there is the same danger of overemphasizing psychology as there is of attaching too much importance to a strictly philosophical treatment. For example, in the study of the enjoyment of music, it may be useful for the understanding of certain aspects of that enjoyment to have an enumeration and description of the bodily sensations during such an experience, but such an enumeration cannot entirely satisfy one who is making an æsthetic study of music. The extreme has been reached in books such as Grant Allen's *Physiological Æsthetics*, where one learns about nerve actions and the psychology of pleasure and pain in general, but is left in ignorance regarding most of the prob-

---

[1] See L. M. Phillipps' *Art and Environment.*

lems of æsthetic enjoyment which have true pragmatic value, especially that of the essential difference between the æsthetic attitude and other forms of pleasurable reactions. More will be said upon this point when we come to the general subject of pleasure. A psycho-physiological book of such a nature has value, in that it describes certain phases of the general problem, but in itself it brings the reader very little closer to beauty.

As regards the objective treatment, namely, the study of the arrangements embodied in the object of enjoyment which produces various æsthetic effects, little explanation is necessary. The danger here has been to under-, rather than to over-estimate its importance, and this is one of the chief causes of the frequently non-empirical character of æsthetics. In modern times, however, it has been recognized that slight differences in arrangement are of great importance to the æsthetic attitude, for example, in the framing and placing of pictures, in the isolation of statues from their surroundings, and in the scenic arrangement of the drama—to mention only a few well-known instances.

§ 4. The Æsthetic Appreciation of Nature

A study of æsthetics should include painting, the industrial arts, sculpture, architecture, literature, the drama, including certain factors of the comic and tragic, music, dancing, and natural beauty; in short, it is concerned with the æsthetic attitude wherever it is found. The fields of inquiry just mentioned are accepted by most æstheticians. The inclusion of natural beauty, however, has at times led to misunderstanding and requires further explanation. Professor Sully has stated that "Some contemplation and appreciation of the beautiful aspects of nature is not only prior in time to art, but is a condition of its genesis. The enjoyment of the pleasing aspects of land and sea, of mountain and dale, of the innumerable organic forms, has steadily grown with the development of culture; and this growth, though undoubtedly aided by that of the feeling for art—especially painting and poetry—is to a large extent independent of it."[1] Some, however, have not considered that natural beauty is an æsthetic object in the same sense as a work of art. For example, it has been stated that the pleasure in viewing a marble group of a wrestling match is altogether different from that obtained in witnessing the actual struggle in the ring. It probably is, but it is not necessarily so, as will be shown later. The misunderstanding has arisen in part from a false distinction between natural beauty and a work of art, namely, that in the appreciation of the one we have a sense of illusion that is absent in the other.[2] In the first place, this is not true. The sense of illusion may not be present in either case, or it may be present in both. The real distinction, if there happens to

[1] Article on "Æsthetics" in the *Encyclopedia Britannica*, 11th edition, p. 281. See also E. F. Carritt's *The Theory of Beauty*, pp. 35 *et seq*.

[2] Konrad Lange, *Das Wesen der Kunst*, Vol. I, pp. 82 *et seq*.

be any, must be sought in the attitude of the observer rather than in the object of contemplation.

It has also been asserted that man is not æsthetically active in regard to nature; that he is given no opportunity to show his creative ability and artistic talent. The truth is that the mind is usually more active in a creative sense in the appreciation of nature than in the enjoyment of a finished work of art. In the latter case, certain definite and fixed arrangements are presented, which one is supposed to accept, while in the appreciation of nature, one is left relatively free to form one's own combinations.

In every perception, there is a selection of certain parts of our environment to the exclusion of others. We perceive those things to which we are especially adapted and this adaptation depends in large part upon our own nature. It is not necessary that everything that is before us should be perceived. Suppose that several men are tramping through the fields. One of them will perceive a group of oak trees with green leaves outlined distinctly against the sky, a flock of sheep, a ragged shepherd, and perhaps a rising moon. The objects stand out in minute detail and sharp relief. He does not actually see them in this way, but his imagination supplies for his perception a memory picture of them as he has previously perceived them under conditions more favorable for revealing their true outlines. Another, viewing the same scene, will perceive the oaks, but the leaves melt softly into the gray sky, and instead of a group of sheep standing out separate and distinct, he will perceive an irregular brown-colored mass and over all a cloud of dust which tints the atmosphere and veils the scene in mystery. The perception in the second case may, with a slight stretching of the term, be called a work of art, and if the observer is skilled in the technique and the power of expression he can reproduce it as he has seen it and to a certain extent enjoy his own æsthetic reaction. Indeed, it seems hardly necessary to add that the study of the appreciation of natural beauty is necessary if we are to understand the first stage of artistic creation. It is in such contemplation that the artist and appreciator are one.

The creative art impulse is present when, as so frequently happens, we neglect this object and include that in our perception, in order to obtain a more pleasing impression, when we relate groups that have no objective bonds, thus achieving a higher unity, and obeying the essential rule for true æsthetic composition. It is not mere chance that in our half-dreamy contemplation of a landscape we are entirely oblivious of the distracting features. Our actual perception depends upon our momentary mood, upon the nature of our adjustment at the time. If we are worried over some insistent problem, it is possible for us to walk through a wood without a single æsthetic reaction

—through the same wood that had previously seemed an object of ravishing beauty.

Although our attitude toward the world is constantly changing it is an important fact that the particular adjustment called æsthetic can, through practice, become a dominant one. The poet, the painter, the musician, come more and more to abstract from their surroundings those features only which pertain to their special arts until, eventually, the world means, for them, a harmony of colors, shapes, sounds and rhythms. The sea reflects the light and shade of human passions. The song of the birds appeals to the tenderest emotions. The sound of words has value for its own sake, and even the tap of the stone-cutter's hammer or the clatter of tired horses' feet becomes the motive for some vital theme.

An example of the change in perception according to the attitude of the observer will make clear what is meant by the influence of thought and mood and individual characteristics upon the object of æsthetic pleasure, for it is to the laws of perception that we must turn for the fundamental facts necessary to an understanding of both appreciation and creation.

If we observe the horizontal and the perpendicular lines comprising Figure 1, we notice that they form different figures according to the direction of our attention. We can perceive a square divided into 25 smaller squares, every square bearing the same relation to every other square. Or, still

observing Figure 1, we can perceive a central
cross as indicated in Figure 2, or a diagonal cross
as in Figure 3. We can even perceive differences
of depth in Figure 1, if we set ourselves to perceive
them.[1] The squares, for example, which form the
cross, may appear to lie closer to the observer than
the other squares. They may also seem larger
than the others. Many other combinations can
be made, and as the object has remained the same,

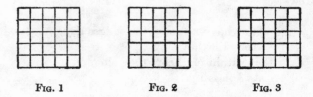

Fig. 1   Fig. 2   Fig. 3

it will be readily granted that the difference has
depended entirely upon the attitude of the observer, or to use a less technical term, upon what
the observer desires to see. We can observe the
same process at work, in more complicated situations, such as solving picture puzzles. When we
are directed to find a hidden figure we can perceive a system of lines, either as the leaves of an
oak tree, or as the outline of a boy.

Ordinarily, in perception we are not aware of the
rôle that our own attitude or personality plays,
for the reason that we are concerned chiefly with
the meaning which has been conveyed, the form

---

[1] Figures 2 and 3 represent the perceptions we obtain when viewing Figure
1 under these different directions of attention.

as actually perceived acting merely as a symbol for the meaning reaction, and being in itself of little importance to us. Such an analysis may seem to some too materialistic a manner of describing the underlying process of what they may prefer to call the response of the soul to the beauties of nature. The subjective aspect of the beauty of things has not escaped the artists, who have expressed the idea in more poetic though less scientific terms.

> "They have no song, the sedges dry,
>   And still they sing.
> It is within my heart they sing,
>   As I pass by.
>
> Within my breast they touch a string,
>   They wake a sigh.
> There is but sound of sedges dry;
>   In me they sing." [1]

To those who have not a preconceived theory concerning art a defense of the study of natural beauty will seem, to some extent at least, superfluous. For some, indeed, nature is the only object that arouses an æsthetic emotion, and it seems false, at least from a psychological point of view, to hold that such pleasure differs from that obtained from the contemplation of a picture or symphony. It is true, however, that our responses to nature are more frequently non-

[1] George Meredith, "Song of the Songless."

æsthetic than æsthetic, owing to the urgency of the practical demands of life. The difference between these two attitudes toward things about us, whether natural or artificial, will form the main thesis of this book.

CHAPTER II

THE SCIENCE OF BEAUTY AND UGLINESS

§ 1. DEFINITION OF ÆSTHETICS

THERE is considerable difference of opinion regarding the definition of æsthetics. While most definitions contain at least a germ of truth, they all too often indicate either a certain confusion in the author's mind, or what is worse, an *a priori* conception of the nature of beauty.

A frequently seen definition is that æsthetics is a philosophy of beauty. It has been shown in the last chapter that the philosophical is only one of the three necessary approaches, if one would have a comprehensive knowledge of the subject. If it happens to be the sole treatment, the study will remain abstract and frequently non-empirical. Instead of starting from experience, such an æsthetics begins with an ideal concept deduced from some higher principle, and attempts to force beauty into the mold thus formed. By way of illustrating such a method, the following example may be supposed: beautiful objects are a part of the Divine Spirit, which is non-spatial in character: it follows that all beautiful objects must be non-spatial. Music can therefore be included in that category, but fine arts must be banished from the realm of beauty; which conclusion is palpably absurd, though entirely consistent with the theory. It is the form of approach which is sometimes to be found in other fields, such as government, where it has been maintained by some that it is in the nature of a State that it cannot commit suicide, and that therefore a State is justified in employing every possible means for its self-preservation. This *a priori* form of æsthetics has been termed by Fechner an æsthetics "from above" in contrast to æsthetics "from below." [1] The latter deals with the facts as they are discoverable in experience and from these it deduces its laws. This is the method of science and there is nothing in the nature of beauty that precludes such treatment.

In truth, the ideal of æsthetics should be a vigorously scientific one, if it is to keep in touch with reality and serve the needs of those who are searching for a wider experience. Experiments may be conducted in æsthetics just as in any other science—a fact which Fechner pointed out in 1871. [2] From the data gathered in this way, as well as from the study of works of art, from the biographies and autobiographies of artists, from anthropological investigations, from the history of art, and from the psychology of appreciation,

[1] *Vorschule der Æsthetik*, p. 1.

[2] Fechner published data from experiments in æsthetics in his article "Ueber die Frage des Goldnen Schnittes" in Weigels *Archiv* in 1865, but it was not until 1871 that he discussed, in his "Zur Experimentalen Æsthetik," the general application of experimental methods in æsthetics (*Vorschule der Æsthetik*, p. 5).

etc., the various laws can be deduced. In this way, certain rules are obtained which aid the development of art, or act as guides for the appreciation of beauty.

It must be remembered, however, that these rules or norms have been deduced from a limited number of facts, and must be changed if they cease to correspond to reality. They are neither more nor less absolute than are any other generalizations from the facts of nature, which at best remain tentative and subject to change. We should aim, therefore, to obtain definite and established rules, that is, reliable generalizations as against *a priori* rules on the one extreme and an accumulation and enumeration of isolated facts on the other, which at best must leave the mind in a state of bewilderment. In other words, we cannot assert dogmatically that art must develop in this or that way. Experience has shown that art will not be commanded, that it bends to no dogmatism. One cannot even agree with the æsthetician who states that "Philosophy must lay down what Beauty has to do," even though it is added that "psychology must deal with the various means through which this end is to be reached." [1] There are some laws, however, which are founded upon such fundamental facts of the human mind that they can be considered, for practical purposes, firmly established. For example, it does seem from what we know of perception that its chief characteristic is unifica-

[1] Puffer, *Psychology of Beauty*, pp. 37–38.

tion. It is through this unification of the object, this relating of its parts one to another, that it is grasped by the mind. There is in this an economy of effort which is essential to mental development. Therefore, it is reasonable to expect that an arrangement of the elements of an object of contemplation which aids this unification will meet the requirements of the mind better and be more acceptable than an arrangement which does not do so. Unity can, therefore, be considered a firmly established principle of beauty. However, such a general law as this must be very carefully applied, for it is found that under certain conditions and in order to produce certain effects, what seems to be somewhat less than the highest degree of unity is demanded. It may even happen that the human mind will change in its future development, and that unity will no longer be essential. If so, one will see art forms change in spite of laws. It will also be shown later that psychology has discovered certain laws in regard to the communication of ideas. So long as art desires to communicate and so long as these laws of mind hold, art will have to conform to them.

These examples have been given to show both that there is in æsthetics a certain background for prophecy as to the permanency of modern movements in art and that there are practical rules for the control of our own artistic development in creation. Our prophecies are also made more reliable and our control over ourselves strengthened by a knowledge of the reason for changes when such occur, and of the causes fundamental to the formulation of rules. The purely inductive nature of such knowledge, however, cannot be too much emphazised if æsthetics is to remain a living science. Many rules which had seemed inviolable have been deserted by art, as for instance, the neglect of the canon of unity of time in the drama, and yet the enjoyment has been as great if not greater. Conditions have changed. New experiences have been introduced, and the mind having become accustomed to a new adjustment, has ceased to find such unity a *sine qua non* of æsthetic enjoyment, in fact at times has welcomed its infraction.

To repeat, it should be the legitimate aim of æsthetics to generalize and to use the results of such generalization as a guide, but the rules thus obtained must be continually tested in experience, and altered according to the conditions thus found. In actual practice, it is found that there is an interplay between the rules and æsthetic development. The rules are the conservative forces which at times guide that development, but which in turn are changed by it.

This view of the nature of rules is the same as that held in modern ethics, which considers the laws of conduct not as divine and unalterable and to which all action must submit, but as a result of the play of human forces, as generalizations from existing conditions, and only of value in so far as they recognize the needs of the race as shown by the race's own development. The similarity between ethics and æsthetics in this respect is illuminating, because both have been considered at times normative sciences. "Thou shalt" and "Duty must" were the patterns upon which the rules were shaped. As the rules have just been described above, however, they conform to the modern conception of science and should be considered a part of it.

Assuming then that æsthetics is a science rather than a philosophy, it remains for us to determine the subject of the science. Professor Sully has written that æsthetics is "a branch of study variously defined as the philosophy or science of the beautiful, of taste or of fine arts." [1] "Taste" is a very broad term. It emphasizes the subjective or purely psychological side of beauty, is ambiguous, and omits the creative act. "The fine arts" is too limiting in its meaning, and even if used in its broadest sense it neglects nature and the act of appreciation. "Beauty" is the term most frequently used, and is best suited to cover what is considered in this treatise the subject of study.

The definition which seems to be most in accord with the present treatise is that by Sir Sidney Colvin which states that "the name æsthetics is intended to designate a scientific doctrine or account of beauty, in nature and art, and of the

[1] *Encyclopedia Britannica,* 11th edition, article on "Æsthetics."

faculty for enjoying and for originating beauty which exists in man." [1]

If only the term "beauty" is used, however, the fact might be overlooked that its opposite, ugliness, involves to an equal degree the æsthetic attitude, and should therefore be expressed rather than merely implied in the definition.[2] The definition of æsthetics may therefore be briefly stated as *the science of beauty and ugliness.* The aim of this treatise will be to put meaning behind these terms.

§ 2. PLEASURE AND PAIN

A mistake that has frequently been made is to identify beauty and ugliness with pleasure and pain. That beauty does give pleasure and ugliness pain cannot be denied. The mistake lies in calling all pleasure æsthetic pleasure. Yet there are psychologists who have considered that they were dealing with æsthetics as soon as they commenced a chapter upon pleasure or an experiment upon the affective states.

Dr. Marshall thinks "that æsthetics may with propriety be considered as a branch of hedonics; as being dependent directly upon pleasure laws and indirectly therefore upon the laws of pain." [3] Consequently he devotes the greater part of his book to a description of the physical basis of pleasure and pain. He does not, however, fall into

---

[1] *Encyclopedia Britannica,* 9th edition, article on "Fine Arts."

[2] Lipps writes (*Æsthetik,* vol. 1, p. 6): "The study of beauty involves a study of its counterpart, ugliness."

[3] *Pain, Pleasure and Æsthetics,* p. 299.

the error of believing that all pleasures are æsthetic, for according to him 'That object is to be considered beautiful which produces a psychosis that is permanently pleasurable in revival. Each pleasure may form an element of impression in an æsthetic complex; but only those pleasures are judged to be æsthetic which (relatively speaking) are permanently pleasurable in memory, the non-æsthetic, so-called, pleasures of memory being merely pleasures in name, psychoses non-pleasurable in themselves in revival, but to which, for one reason or another, the word 'pleasure' still clings."[1] It is quite probable that those of artistic tastes through their great interest in beauty find that pleasure which is derived from objects of art is more lasting than other pleasures, but there is considerable individual variation in this regard. Undoubtedly there are those who will insist that the pleasure caused by the news of some great success is more permanent than that derived from a picture, and yet, unless we desire to argue *ex definitione*, as Dr. Marshall does, in the last part of the sentence just quoted, we can hardly deny that they obtain some idea, although perhaps a very slight one, of the beauty of pictures.

Most writers have like Dr. Marshall attempted some differentiation of æsthetic pleasure from mere sensuous pleasure. One of the frequent and very superficial distinctions is that between the so-called lower and higher senses. Such a theory as-

---

[1] *Op. cit.*, p. 110. (Italics in original have been omitted.)

serts that one enjoys æsthetically the impressions which one receives through the eye and ear, and sensuously those which are received through the nose, mouth, and skin. It is a fact that we are more likely to be æsthetically moved through the enjoyment of a picture than through the pleasure derived from the touch of certain fabrics, or the taste blends of a meal, for reasons that will be explained later, but it must be insisted upon that the latter may have an æsthetic quality, and in fact does have more frequently than some like to admit, who are influenced by a certain odium which has attached itself for various reasons to what is experienced through these lower senses. Because certain of these experiences are considered vulgar, they have all fallen in the scale of values. It would indeed make the problem simpler if it were agreed that all pleasures are æsthetic that are experienced through the higher senses. It would then only be necessary to ask whether the experience was one of pleasure or pain, and what senses were involved. If for example, we were puzzled as to whether we were maintaining a truly æsthetic attitude toward a picture, we should merely have to ask whether it gave us pleasure; if so, the attitude could be called an æsthetic one. This solution probably satisfies some persons. It does not, however, enable us to decide the æsthetic values of various forms of the drama, the effect of violent emotions in the appreciation of art, the function of realism, the relation of content and form, and a multitude of similar questions which are involved in the fundamental problem of the nature of beauty. It would be a clear-cut definition and easy of application, but a very dull instrument for the purpose, and of as much practical value as is Kant's categorical imperative in ethics and jurisprudence.

Grant Allen, who has limited æsthetic pleasure to the higher senses, has given an ingenious reason for so doing. He maintains that æsthetic pleasure is the result of normal activity "not directly connected with life-serving functions of the nervous system." [1] The lower senses are connected with these functions, therefore, they cannot transmit an æsthetic experience, although he suggests that there is "a faint approach to the æsthetic level in tastes of the pure gustatory class, the sweets and the bitters." Before passing to the main criticism it should be remarked that it is impossible to understand the meaning of "faint approach." An experience is either æsthetic or not æsthetic. There is no third possibility.

We shall see later the rôle that such life-serving functions play in disturbing the æsthetic attitude, but it must be asked whether they always have to be a disturbing factor, and—what is pertinent to the present discussion—whether life-serving functions are limited to the lower senses. When one enters a picture gallery after the fatigue and worry of a busy day and is transported into another world, as it is so frequently termed, can one

[1] *Physiological Æsthetics*, p. 34.

dogmatically state that the glow of pleasure, quickening of the pulse, and change in breathing are not life-giving? Yet the impression is through the eye; so that one is in the predicament of having to decide whether it is an æsthetic pleasure because it is a visual one, or non-æsthetic because it is life-serving. Attention should also be called to the fact, if the objection is raised that Allen did not mean life-giving in the sense used above, that many of the experiences obtained through the lower senses, as for example, olfactory and muscular sensations, are even less life-giving than the reaction to pictures.

Lange has pointed out [1] that we cannot use this distinction between the senses as our criterion for beauty, inasmuch as we experience pleasure from many things perceived visually which we should not call artistic. He also rightfully maintains that the arousal of pleasure is not in itself a criterion of a work of art, and that the real distinction must be sought in the mental processes accompanying such pleasure. His main criterion, namely that of illusion, will be criticised later. He is particularly interesting at this point as an instance of that class of æstheticians which assigns more importance to distinguishing objects which afford higher or æsthetic pleasure from those which produce a lower form of enjoyment, than to an analysis of the total æsthetic attitude. The danger in the method of such writers is that in classifying

[1] *Das Wesen der Kunst,* Vol. I, p. 73.

this experience as æsthetic and that as non-æsthetic, they lead one to suppose that the relation between the object of appreciation and the observer is constant; in short that the mind will always react to the object in the same way. The true nature of beauty cannot be ascertained by comparing a display of fireworks, as such, with a painting by Titian, or the music of an Æolian harp with the rendering of a concerto by Joachim upon a Stradivarius.[1] All that is gained is the knowledge that some objects are in general more likely to arouse the idea of beauty than others. For most persons, cookery does not become an object of beauty, but it may on occasion; and who will deny an æsthetic experience to the Englishman who, in describing a remarkable dinner he had attended, was moved to ecstatic expression by the harmony of wines and viands, or to the Frenchman who dilated upon the beauty of a certain combination of liqueurs?

§ 3. THE VARIOUS ATTITUDES TOWARD THE ENVIRONMENT

The possibility of various attitudes toward nature, together with the unifying function of perception, has previously been described. One may contemplate the stars in the heavens with the purely scientific interest of an astronomer or may delight in the beauty of the myriads of flickering points in the unified pattern which seems to unfold

[1] *Op. cit.*, Vol. I, p. 75.

before one's gaze. A football game is not generally considered an object of beauty, yet it is quite conceivable that an expert may be so thrilled by the smoothness of the play and by the exact execution of the well-drilled attack that for the moment even the thought of victory will have no place in his consciousness. The exclamation "Beautiful!" which escapes his lips will have been used in a sense as legitimate as the most critical purist can desire.

For the casual observer, standing in a railroad station and watching the approach of a train, the engine will probably be merely a means of locomotion. When, however, the engineer, or an individual who thoroughly understands engines, observes the smooth-running machinery and the manner in which the functions of the various parts are united into an organic whole which appears almost human, the pleasure obtained will be truly æsthetic. It may seem to some a stretching of the meaning of the word, to speak of a beautiful surgical operation, yet the surgeon has a very distinct æsthetic pleasure in an operation that has been accomplished in accordance with his highest desires. It was a difficult task which has been smoothly performed.

In connection with the above examples, the fact of unification should be emphasized, for, as will be seen later, experience of unity is fundamental to æsthetic pleasure. As some degree of unity can always be obtained no matter what the object,

every situation contains at least the latent possibility of arousing such a pleasure. As Professor
R. M. Ogden has stated "There should be . . .
nothing in all human experience toward which one
cannot maintain an æsthetic attitude. Nature
in all the manifoldness of her stimuli, emotions
in all degrees of violence, possess æsthetic elements
which, under favorable conditions, may be made
dominant, and their attendant states appreciated
with quiet and repose." [1]

Thus far, we have used the word object to denote
a thing such as a book or a tree, but the term is
also used in the sense of an æsthetic object, a
useful object, a scientific object, etc., denoting
the various relations which the thing can have
to the mind which is experiencing it. A book lies
upon the table; one discovers that it is by Ruskin;
the book then becomes a literary object, it arouses
in the mind memories of the great critic, and one
likes or dislikes it according to one's opinion of the
author. If one is a publisher, a thought as to the
number of editions may occur, and its appeal
becomes purely commercial, or it may be the size
and shape of the book and its color which attract
one, and the fact that it is by Ruskin may only
play a part in that the color is found to be appropriate to the contents. The book thus becomes
an æsthetic object.

To exemplify the point further, consider the relations that a crystal can occupy toward the mind.

[1] "The Esthetic Attitude," *Journal of Philosophy*, etc., 1905, pp. 411–412.

The scientist's interests will be in the angles, hardness, color, etc., as indications of its nature; the psychologist will be interested in the color of the crystal in so far as it is related to problems of physiological optics; and a third individual will find the combination of sparkling colors, as such, of sufficient interest to hold the attention. In accordance with the general use of the term, it is the same object in each case, namely, the crystal, yet in a restricted sense it is a different object to each individual.

These changes are what Vernon Lee appropriately terms the various aspects of things.[1] She describes the attitude of three men viewing a certain landscape, and she shows how different is its appeal to the landowner, to the scientist, and to the æsthetician. We have seen above that we do not need three separate minds in order to have a change in the appeal. The same mind reacts differently, according to the mood and the setting. A familiar way of stating the same fact is that the object has different meanings for different individuals and situations. Psychologically it may be stated that the organism adopts different reaction patterns toward the same object. In the example of the three men viewing the landscape, the landowner may run his eye over the edge of the field in an attempt to estimate its extent and may at the same time repeat to himself the value per acre of such land. That action together with con-

[1] *The Beautiful*, pp. 8–21.

comitant associated tendencies becomes for the moment his aspect of the situation. The geologist may glance over the same ridge in search of a certain kind of rock, while images, more or less distinct, of the quality of the rock sought may be in his mind; while the artist in ignorance of his companion's thoughts may be sketching in the air with his hand the outline of the hill as he looks over the same scene. Each one is pleased with his view, each one has in one sense the same object of contemplation, and yet the three men are as far apart in their thoughts as they could be. The difference does not lie in the fact that pleasure is aroused or that there is an object of a particular quality, nor even in subtle differences in feeling, for the only two qualities of feeling that exist, according to the opinion of the majority of psychologists, are pleasure and displeasure. The difference must be sought in the total situation. In each case, there is a different relation between the object and the mind. One of these relations with its accompanying pleasure or pain is the æsthetic relation, and the total situation is called beautiful or ugly; therefore it is not possible to discover the nature of beauty and ugliness by the examination of objects alone, or of the sensations and feelings aroused, but by an analysis of the relation, and this will form the subject of the next chapter.

CHAPTER III

THE ÆSTHETIC ATTITUDE

§ 1. Concerning Theories of Beauty

Fundamental to an understanding of the æsthetic relation is a clear knowledge of the attitude of the observer during æsthetic enjoyment. In order, however, to understand the point of view to be expounded here, it will first be necessary to review and criticise briefly a few representative theories. It will be found that there is a degree of similarity in all of them. In fact, some seem at first glance so similar that essential differences are often overlooked. Also, they have, for the most part, contained a certain amount of truth which has made them more or less acceptable, but on examination it will be found that the terms are so vague and used so loosely that they may mean everything or nothing. Their authors, instead of explaining them fully in psychological terms, have left them so ambiguous that often they are mere words which one interprets according to one's own inclination. Instead of suggestive words, one should be given the psychological content behind them with sufficient clearness to enable one to adjust oneself in the sense intended.

§ 2. Absence of Utility and Purpose

The most frequently and generally accepted concept, and the one that the majority of æstheticians

have included in their definitions, from the time
of the Greek philosophers, is that of the utter
absence of utility. We value most things for what
we can do with them, for the benefit we derive
from them, but in the enjoyment of art, according
to this theory, all such materialistic thoughts are
absent. The object of beauty is pleasing in itself.

Kant excluded even the idea of perfection from
the judgment of what he termed "free beauty,"
since utility is involved in perfection. This "free
beauty" is obtained only in pure designs such as
the arabesque. Horses or buildings, etc., can only
give us "appendant" beauty since they involve
the idea of perfection.[1] In order to make beauty
entirely "free" there should not even be interest
in the possession of the object. It should be im-
material whether we own a picture or whether it is
in a public gallery; in fact, the picture should be
preferred in a public gallery so far as the real
æsthetic enjoyment is concerned. There is no
doubt that ideas of use, perfection, possession,
etc., interfere with, even if they do not preclude
the perception of beauty. We want to know, however, why such ideas are in any way opposed to an
æsthetic attitude; why it may be easier to enjoy
a picture in a spirit more truly æsthetic in a gallery than in our own house. It is desired to know
what is the difference in the psychological attitude
under these various conditions and this involves

[1] See Kant's *Critique of Æsthetic Judgment*, translated by J. C. Meredith,
pp. 69–74.

a knowledge of what is meant psychologically by the enjoyment of a thing for itself.

Further, the terms useful and non-useful, although suggesting a satisfactory solution, do not clearly separate the æsthetic from the non-æsthetic, for it will be readily admitted that in the broad sense of the word the æsthetic itself is extremely useful.

The term non-practical is also frequently used to describe the æsthetic relation, but just as in the case of the term useful we want to know more clearly what is meant. It might readily be asked whether an artist in painting a picture for the market was not highly practical. Even if he were merely painting it for the annual *Salon* and had no other thought but his reputation in mind, he might still be considered to be deserving of that epithet "practical," which is supposed to be derogatory when applied to æsthetic endeavor.

To say that things are pleasing in themselves, or as it is still more vaguely expressed, that beauty is self-contained, not only conveys no knowledge of the attitude, but by its very phraseology discourages a search beyond the object of beauty into the subjective realm of psychological facts.

An obvious implication in the theory of the absence of utility is that of absence of purpose and of desire. Both concepts can be dismissed with a word. There is absence of purpose except the purpose of creation or enjoyment of the beautiful, and absence of desire except that one desires with all one's soul the experience called beautiful. As Mr. E. F. Carritt expresses it: "There is more truth in the common negative description that beauty is what pleases apart from desire. But this needs considerable qualification and explanation. Those to whom beauty means most do in fact desire it, though only for purposes of contemplation, just as they desire food though only for eating; and both appetites may, by starvation, become cravings. What is meant would probably be better expressed by saying that beauty is what pleases in the mere contemplation.[1] This would probably cover some things not usually or properly thought beautiful, and it certainly throws little light upon the nature of beauty; but as a rough description it might serve."[2] As Mr. Carritt indicates, such a definition is a good starting point, but it is necessary to know more fully what is meant by mere contemplation. In short, those who have the power to enjoy beauty, and who have to a certain extent examined their attitude, especially those who have made some study of the philosophy of art, will undoubtedly see a kernel of truth in all of these definitions, but it may be surmised that they will find them only vaguely descriptive of their true experience, and that those who have been less analytical or who have been little in touch with art, will have difficulty in understanding them without further explanation.

[1] This is the definition of Thomas Aquinas: "Id cujus ipsa apprehensio placet" (Summa, Ia, 2 oe, quæst. 27, art. 1).

[2] *Theory of Beauty*, pp. 8–9.

§ 3. Detachment and Isolation

Three authors have recently made progress
toward a more complete description of beauty, by
attempting an analysis of the æsthetic relation:
Münsterberg, Puffer, and Bullough. Münsterberg's theory has offered useful suggestions, but
his concepts, though clearer than those previously
mentioned, are still sufficiently vague to leave
room for serious misunderstanding. He speaks of
the detachment of the subject and the isolation of
the object, thus emphasizing the relational aspect
of beauty, although it must be added that this was
probably not his intention as he would scarcely
have subscribed to a theory which was so little in
accord with his general philosophical tendencies.
In describing his views, he indicates the difference
between the attitude of the scientist and that of the
appreciator of beauty. The scientist searches
always for the cause and effect of things; in so doing, he must relate objects to their surroundings,
and to the past, and the future. His interest is not
entirely in the object as such but goes beyond it.
In the case of beauty, however, Münsterberg asks,
"Is it not possible to give the whole of our mind
to the presentation of the one thing alone with all
that it gives us, with all that it shows and suggests, while the world about it and the world
around us, are forgotten?" [1] Not only is it possible, but according to him it is essential if we are

[1] Principles of Art Education, p. 19.

to know beauty. "If you really want the thing itself, there is only one way to get it. You must separate it from everything else, you must disconnect it from the mind so that nothing else but this one presentation fills the mind, so that there remains no room for anything beside it. If that ever can be reached, the result must be clear: for the object it means complete isolation; for the subject, it means complete repose in the object, and that is complete satisfaction with the object; and that is, finally, merely another name for the enjoyment of beauty." [1]

Very good, but when one considers the words more closely, one is led to ask for further knowledge of detachment. Is it the neglect of what surrounds the work of art? Then that is a general attitude whenever one gives anything one's entire attention. Is it detachment from everything that does not directly concern the object? If so, that would include detachment from all that makes up the personality of the observer. It would imply detachment from one's self, and that this does not take place will be shown later, for the fact is that the subconscious desires and wishes that form the self, instead of being detached from experience, are very essential for a deep and vital appreciation of beauty. Without the appeal to one's underlying tendencies, there would be the cold intellectual judgment which as closely resembles æsthetic pleasure as the light from an arc lamp does

[1] *Op. cit.*, p. 20.

a sunset. Nor should one so completely isolate an object that the idea of causal connection is lost, for it is largely through the knowledge of this relation that the object gains meaning, and even in the experience of beauty meaning is essential.

It may be said in defense of this theory of "detachment" that it merely means that when the observer is fully conscious of the causal relation he loses his æsthetic attitude. If the theory does mean that, then, in a certain sense, it is true, and yet this very causal relation, as for example the effect of social forces in the drama, may very well be the central object of æsthetic contemplation. Even if this is not conceded, still a non-awareness of causal relations cannot be the criterion of æsthetic appreciation, since such non-awareness is the most usual attitude toward the objects of experience. When one sees an apple fall from the tree, it is more likely that one's thought will be to pick it up, rather than to consider the law of gravity or the manner of reflection of the ether waves from its rosy cheeks.

To say that the object should be completely isolated has little practical value without further information derived from an analysis of the attitude we call æsthetic. The object, of course, should be separated from all that detracts from one's contemplation, but what the limits of such isolation should be are not indicated in these general terms. We cannot say that when we enjoy a picture our attention should be entirely centered on the canvas and that nothing beyond should play any part in our attitude. The surroundings are necessarily of influence and either add to or detract from our total enjoyment. No one would pretend that it is a matter of indifference how a picture is hung in a gallery. Even the frame, which through its function of restricting the gaze, isolates the object and in consequence aids our æsthetic perception, must itself be included as a factor in the total harmonious effect. Yet it might readily be considered merely the instrument for this isolation and be excluded from consideration, if we had nothing but the bare concept of isolation to guide us.

It is recognized that Münsterberg undoubtedly did not desire to be taken so literally. This criticism, trivial in itself, is given merely to show how difficult it is to determine, by the application of so general a concept as isolation, just what should be considered to belong to the work of art. A further difficulty is that even though Münsterberg has stated that isolation is the result of that attitude he called detachment, one cannot be quite sure from the examples he has given whether isolation is the result of detachment, or detachment the result of isolation. It is a distinct gain that he has emphasized the psychological factors, but it still remains to explain more fully what these are before the meaning of the terms is sufficiently clear to exclude deductions that are contrary to actual experience.

It may be admitted, then, that there are in the two words, detachment and isolation, some valuable suggestions. When, however, Münsterberg says that there is repose in the object of æsthetic enjoyment, he most decidedly contradicts the facts. It has been shown that all perception—and æsthetic experience certainly falls under that term—involves active participation on the part of the observer. This activity is not only a so-called mental activity such as is experienced in imagination, but is often one of observable bodily movements. A few paragraphs beyond the above quotation, Münsterberg himself, influenced by philosophic considerations which were everywhere his guide, speaks of the isolated object as "an artificial transformation of reality to serve the purpose of our will," [1] words which most surely imply the demand for activity rather than for repose, if the term "will" is to have any meaning. Further, throughout his psychological writings, Münsterberg repeatedly emphasizes the sensations from muscular movements as an essential and integral part of our mental life. His use of the term repose is an example of theory running beyond fact, and has been described here partly as an example of such tendencies, partly because it was an important mistake of his general theory. That it was considered an essential part of his concept of beauty is indicated by the fact that it is much enlarged upon by his pupil, Miss Ethel Puffer.

[1] *Op. cit.,* p. 21.

§ 4. Repose in the Object of Beauty

For Miss Puffer, the loss of the sense of personality is necessary in æsthetic appreciation, and when this is obtained there is also a condition of complete repose. In order to understand what is meant by loss of personality, it is necessary to explain briefly the nature of attention, and what she means by foreground and background of thought. Suppose the attention is concentrated upon some object of perception, but not to such a high degree that there is not also consciousness of certain organic feelings, as for example the beating of the heart, the rhythmical breathing, and the weight of the clothes. A description of such a state of mind would be that the object of perception is in the center of consciousness, and that the ideas of the sensations of a strictly personal nature, which together make up the experience of self, are, as James states, in the fringe of consciousness. Another way of stating it is that there are several levels of attention, and when one is self-conscious it is because one has shifted from the topics of objective interest which were in the center or upper level to others of a more personal nature, which were in the lower level or fringe. After a period of self-consciousness, there is likely to be a shift back to other interests. This change of interest from center to fringe of consciousness is, for Miss Puffer, a lack of repose.

In order to illustrate her theory of repose Miss

Puffer describes, however, instances such as hypnotic trances and ecstatic states of religious fanatics, where all sense of personality disappears. When we focus our attention upon a bright button the intense light reflected from it will soon occupy our consciousness to the exclusion of everything else. It is then that one reposes in the object, for there is at such times no wandering back and forth between foreground and background, the term wandering being used in a vague, metaphorical sense. It is such a mental state that the mystics attain when they feel themselves one with God. "The mystic, then, need only shut his senses to the world, and contemplate the One." [1] This, according to Miss Puffer, is perfect repose, and it is this state that is found in the contemplation of beauty. Such a condition is what is known psychologically as a one-level state of attention. It is present whenever we are entirely interested in what we are doing, whether we are listening to a symphony or sharpening a lead pencil, and is not peculiar to the contemplation of beauty. As to the loss of the feeling of personality, this is the most frequent condition of one's conscious state. Contrary to the popular view, which generally involves a confusion between consciousness and self-consciousness, it is relatively seldom that one is self-conscious.

It will be necessary, then, to seek beyond the loss of self as thus described, in order to find the distinguishing factors of the æsthetic relation; and this

[1] *Psychology of Beauty*, p. 76.

applies equally to the sense of repose, for no one
can pretend to identify enjoyment of beauty with
a hypnotic trance or a religious excursion into
Nirvana.

An understanding of the nature of this repose
is made more difficult by the introduction of another kind of repose, produced by the balance of
impulses, and it is nowhere made clear what is the
relation between this form and that of the repose of
attention. In fact, one is led to believe that they
are identical, the truth being, however, that they
are two totally different things. The one form is a
fact and essential to æsthetic enjoyment, but no
more so than to any other complete perception.
The presence of the other form, that is, repose
through balance, would entirely prevent appreciation. Miss Puffer describes it thus: ". . . it
may be said that the unity of the object is constituted just by the inhibition of all tendency to
movement through the balance or centrality of
impulses suggested by it. In other words, the
balance of impulses makes us feel the object a
unity. And this balance of impulses, this inhibition of movement, corresponding to unity, is what
we know as æsthetic repose." [1] It will be readily
seen that such repose brought about by the balance
of impulses suggested by the object is very different from the repose of a concentrated attention
that has ceased to travel from foreground, that
is the object, to the background, which is the per-

[1] *Op. cit.*, p. 79.

sonality. Yet in the very next line it is stated that "conditions of æsthetic repose and of the loss of self-feeling are the same. In fact, it might be said that, within this realm, the two conceptions are identical." [1]

To return to the balance of impulses, it is difficult to understand how such a balance, which in art is one between forces actually felt as such by the observer, can be called repose. One is hardly in a restful attitude when one is fully cognizant, for example, of the "tension of conflict, the balance of emotion," etc.,[2] in the drama. Such a state is as much repose as is that of the participants in an equally balanced tug-of-war. It is a curious fact that the actual empirical descriptions of the enjoyment of beauty given by the author contradict her idea of repose. It is difficult to see, for example, how the statement concerning repose quoted above could have been preceded by the following without the inconsistency being observed: "The depth of æsthetic feeling lies . . . in him who creates the drama again with the poet, who lives over again in himself each of the thrills of emotion passing before him, and loses himself in their web. The object is a unity or our *whirling* circle of impulses, as you like to phrase it." [3] Or this: "The real ground of the possibility of a momentary self-annihilation lies in the fact that all incitements to

---

[1] *Op. cit.*, p. 79.
[2] *Ibid.*, p. 243.
[3] *Ibid.*, pp. 78–79. (Italics not in original.)

motor impulses—*except those which belong to the indissoluble ring of the object itself*—have been shut out by the perception of unity to which the æsthetic object (here the drama) has been brought." [1] These descriptions are given here not only because they contradict the idea of repose, but also because they are, with slight qualifications, true and useful ideas of the æsthetic attitude, and it is unfortunate that they should have led to such a mistaken theory.

§ 5. PSYCHICAL DISTANCE

One of the most valuable descriptions of the conditions underlying beauty is that given by Dr. Bullough in his theory of "psychical distance." [2] The term "distance" is used metaphorically and not in the sense of spatial or temporal separation. It may for that reason be misleading to some readers, and further, the phrase "psychical distance" has an unfortunately mystical connotation. In one place, Dr. Bullough uses the term "detachment," but, after all, the name is of little importance, inasmuch as he makes his underlying meaning fairly clear by well-chosen examples.

Let it be supposed that an individual is on a ship during a storm, and there is serious danger of shipwreck. It is quite possible that even in such a situation, a man of artistic temperament would

[1] *Op. cit.*, p. 78. (Italics not in original.)
[2] "'Psychical Distance,' as a Factor in Art and an Æsthetic Principle," *The British Journal of Psychology*, vol. 5, pp. 87–118.

admire the movements of the waves, and the dash
of the spray, entirely oblivious of danger, and with
no concern as to what the high seas may ultimately
do to the ship. Descriptions of such a state of
mind, even in situations of extreme danger, are
frequently found in literature. For Dr. Bullough
there would here be complete psychical distance.
Suddenly, however, a wave larger than any previous one approaches and the artist's muscles set in
preparation to meet the blow. Dr. Bullough
would say that at that instant he has entirely lost
his distance, that is, his æsthetic attitude. It will
now be better understood why Dr. Bullough has
termed the distance "psychical" for it denotes the
mental attitude. In the one instant, the man is
entirely lost in the shape of the wave and its force,
and in the color of the water; in the next, although
he still sees the shape and its color, he is interested
only in his preparation to meet the contingency.

Dr. Bullough derives another illustration from
the play of *Othello*. If a man whose wife has recently been false to him witnesses this play, it
is possible and even probable, that, at the moment
when Othello strangles Desdemona, he will be reminded too vividly of his own marital experiences
and will project these into the scene before him.
Instead of observing the interplay of the dramatic
forces as presented by Shakespeare he will scarcely
fail to imagine his own wife in the place of Desdemona. In so doing he ceases to view the play
æsthetically. An analogous situation actually

occurs in the play of *Hamlet*, in the scene where
Hamlet and the King are spectators of a play within
the play.   When an impersonator of this very
King murderously pours poison into the ear of the
late King, who was Hamlet's father, both Hamlet
and the present King are too personally touched,
their private thoughts and emotions are too deeply
aroused and they cease to live strictly in the play.
Or, as some æstheticians would say, they cease
to "be in the object," or they lose their æsthetic
repose.   As Dr. Bullough would say, they lose
their "psychical distance."

§ 6. COMPLETE PARTICIPATION IN THE OBJECT OF BEAUTY

It is now in place, before proceeding further with
the factors of distance, to explain more fully the
nature of the æsthetic attitude, and it will then
be more clearly seen what place distance has in
such an attitude, for it is not entirely clear from
Dr. Bullough's own description.   When one views
an object æsthetically, one lives in the object in
the sense that one allows oneself to be entirely
swayed by the laws of the object without any opposition upon one's own part.   It is a very active
participation, and the term "passive" can be used
only in the sense that one allows oneself to be led.
What is added through the imagination is prescribed by the totality of the object, and one's
adjustments are shaped accordingly, the object
being allowed in all ways to dictate the manner

of such adjustment. The æsthetic attitude may be likened to rowing downstream with the current and following all of its windings. One is here active in that one moves with the stream, but passive in that one opposes no resistance to the force which is carrying one on. The attitude is lost when one attempts to push upstream or off on the side eddy of one's choice. One is reminded of an illustration by Fidus of children in a boat paddling with the stream who think they are pushing while in reality they are drifting with the current.

What is meant is best shown by the attitude at the drama. Here one follows and lives the acts of each of the players as the plot unfolds, instead of identifying oneself with one actor and, in the eagerness to meet the developing situation, anticipating events contrary to the central idea of the author. In the truly æsthetic participation, one is swayed back and forth by the conflicting forces. One is successively hero, villain, and clown. One awaits the attack with the actor, and does not advance to meet it otherwise than as depicted. If the scene involves the ringing of the church bell, one does not, in one's imagination, stroll toward the church, unless there are indications that it is intended that one should. It may be objected that one frequently allows one's imagination to wander from the plot and to build a plot of one's own. That is true, but then, for the moment, one becomes playwright instead of audience. The artist is bound as well as the audience. He is bound by his own unified plan and so long as he keeps within it, he too is a servant of the characters and walks and talks with them all.

The man who lost his distance at the play of *Othello* by imagining his wife in the place of Desdemona ceased to feel the total conflict in that he became identified with Othello alone and no longer lived in the lines of the playwright. By that act the æsthetic attitude was lost. Actors have often felt flattered by effects upon their audience which were totally unæsthetic. A famous actor delighted to recount an incident which occurred while he was playing *The Middleman*. He was a poor inventor who had used up his last resources and could not obtain sufficient fuel to keep up the furnace fire in which the pottery was being hardened. Only a few moments more and his fortune would have been made. Moved by the excitement of the scene, a man in the gallery threw down fifty cents, shouting, "Here, old man, buy wood with it." This active participation was proof of the realism of the scene, but an actor with ideals of his art would scarcely care to act before an audience composed entirely of such individuals. Such an attitude as that just described is typical of the melodrama where the audience frequently hisses the villain and applauds the hero when it is not warning him of approaching danger; truly an attitude which is highly enjoyable to those concerned. Such participation can, however, scarcely be termed æsthetic, for it is opposing oneself to the tendencies and motives of the play.

Another actor has described the fright of one of the musicians in the orchestra when the actor rushed down the stage toward him in one of his most dramatic scenes. The musician never became accustomed to this scene. Night after night he started back in terror before the onrush of the actor. So pleased was the latter that at the end of the engagement he presented the musician with a box of cigars. It would be difficult for any one in the musician's position to have retained his æsthetic outlook, to have been so occupied by the plot and acting that he would have followed the actor in thought instead of retreating before him; but if that was also the effect upon the rest of the audience, the play could not be considered a success so far as beauty is concerned.

Even applause at critical points of the acting, so annoying to the lover of dramatic art, although an indication of appreciation, is also proof that the audience has for the time lost its distance and slipped away from the purely æsthetic. As an example from the appreciation of nature, one may stand upon the shore in deep enjoyment of the "cold gray mist and the dawn," one may be enchanted by the lines of the waves, the soft spray of the foaming water as it slides up the smooth beach, one may feel the movement of the water and the lines of the beach as it inclines to meet it, and the unity of the total situation. One may become so absorbed in the harmony of lines and color that one is entirely oblivious of the fact that the water has touched one's shoes. It is obvious that when one retreats before the waves one loses one's distance, that the water is no longer a thing of beauty, but a force that is compelling one to withdraw. It cannot be said that the loss of æsthetic attitude is due to the intrusion of the thought of self into consciousness, and for that reason one ceases to "repose" in the object, for one's flight may be so nearly reflex and instantaneous that there is no place or time for self-consciousness. It might be asked whether in the backward movement one were not still living in the scene. To this one may reply that the movements would not be according to any requirement of the scene itself, and they would not be a part of or harmonize with the picture that has been before one as an object of æsthetic enjoyment.

One may enjoy the tone of the bugle call æsthetically and retain one's distance by the contemplation of fundamental tone and overtones. One's usual attitude, however, is a non-æsthetic one; the sound starts a movement the manner of which is in no way prescribed by the sound itself, nor in harmony with it. A group of individuals hearing it will all understand its meaning, but the variations in response may be as great as the number of individuals and the enjoyment may be either in the sound itself, in the manner of response, or in the union of the two.

In entering an art gallery one comes suddenly upon a Greek statue with outstretched hand. There may be an involuntary tendency to put out one's hand under a misapprehension that the statue invites it, but the manner of stretching one's own hand is not indicated by the statue, and there can therefore be no question of the harmony of this movement with the movements as indicated by the lines of the figure. This first surprised attitude, then, is non-æsthetic and in sharp contrast with the attitude assumed when enjoying the beauty of the statue. There is also in this latter attitude the tendency to stretch the arm, but it is in order to feel the full value of the lines of the statue. It is an extension of the arm *with* the arm of the statue and not *toward* it, and thus a movement in harmony with the rest of the statue as intended by the sculptor. A full description of the nature of this participation or empathy is not in question here, but will be discussed in the following chapter. The intention here is merely to make clear the general distinction between the æsthetic and non-æsthetic activities of the observer.

The æsthetic attitude as thus described is diametrically opposed to one's usual attitude toward one's environment, the one which one learns to assume by reason of the struggle for existence. In this latter attitude, we are continually opposing forces. Our organism becomes set or adjusted to meet and overcome obstacles, while, as has been stated above, the æsthetic set is directed toward experiencing in ourselves the various relations which the elements of the object have to one another and not our own independent action in regard to them. Biologically it is the more independent action which is of significance and interest, and for this reason it is for most of us the habitual mode of response. The æsthetic attitude, on the other hand, is not only more unusual, but one that for most individuals has to be cultivated if it is to exist at all in the midst of the opposing and therefore disturbing influences which are always present. We are accustomed to put out our hand in greeting, to retreat from advancing waves, and to brace ourselves against attack. The man who does not seem to have this attitude is considered somewhat abnormal, and the artist who has developed the contrary mode of response belongs to the type so frequently called erratic. If the word "detachment" is understood to mean this latter attitude, then the term may be legitimately used to describe the artistic state of mind.

§ 7. The Feeling of Unreality

It is possible to explain the feeling of unreality which is present in æsthetic experience in terms of that adjustment of the organism which is characteristic of the æsthetic attitude. When we react to the world with our habitual mode of response, things seem real. When there is a derangement, we experience a feeling of unreality, which can become pathological in its extreme form. In certain nervous diseases, there is, through a disorder in the sympathetic nervous system, an absence of the usual emotional response. For example, if there is news of the death of an intimate friend, full meaning of the message is grasped intellectually by the one suffering from such a nervous disorder, but there is an absence of the accustomed emotion. The eyes remain dry, the heart fails to beat more irregularly, and the patient complains that there is a strong sense of unreality, as would be the case if he were witnessing a drama instead of living an experience which is of vital importance to him. Familiar objects no longer call up emotional responses. In fact, the whole world is viewed with indifference. This is what is known as an estrangement from the world of reality. Soldiers have frequently stated that while on the front line, it seemed to them as though they were witnessing a play, that life under shell fire was like a well-staged drama, although they were actually participating in the most vital events that ever involved civilization. The explanation of this experience, and it has been too often corroborated to be doubted, seems to be in the unaccustomed responses that are made. The soldiers have been meeting conditions that they have never had to face before, perhaps not even in their most uncontrolled imaginings, and they must develop a new, and unaccustomed set of adjustments. Their manner of thought changes; generally in

the direction of a doctrine of fatalism which they
embrace in order to maintain their mental balance.
Not only that, but their emotions have been so
often and strongly aroused that they become almost indifferent to the most harrowing scenes,
to horrors that in their ordinary life as peaceful
civilians would have overpowered them.   Their
state is very similar to the pathological one just
described, and a remark that is frequently heard
is that "It is all so strange that I can hardly believe it is real."

The æsthetic attitude (being a non-resisting one)
is not, as previously stated, such an adjustment as
is ordinarily assumed toward the environment.
There is a different motor set, and for that reason
there is present in appreciation a feeling of make-
believe which has given rise to an identification
that is so frequently made between art and play.
It is not meant that this sense of unreality is
vividly in consciousness in æsthetic contemplation.
It is no more strongly represented than is the
feeling of familiarity toward our own clothes or
our accustomed haunts.   We are usually fully
conscious of our familiar surroundings only when
some aspect of them has been changed.[1]

It is this unreality which Professor Konrad
Lange has termed "illusion," and which he has
made the criterion of art, without, however,
searching for its deeper significance.   He writes,
"We conclude . . . that æsthetic enjoyment

---

[1] This is more fully described on page 111.

which a work of art as work of art affords is dependent neither upon the quality of its content nor upon its formal nature, but that it rests entirely upon the strength and vividness of the illusion to which the artist brings us through his art." [1] To Professor Lange, who is concerned only with art and not with beauty in nature, that may have seemed a sufficient definition, but it is not adequate and it entirely fails to explain the æsthetic enjoyment of natural beauty. A knowledge of the psychology of the attitude is first required, and an understanding of the sense of illusion follows. The characteristics of the art object as such are not the only factors of illusion. There will be no sense of illusion in witnessing a play, even though it has all the qualities that are usually favorable to illusion, if we slip from the æsthetic attitude.

The question of realism in art has caused much difficulty because it involves ideas that have appeared hard to reconcile. The dramatic critic asks for "real" situations and "real" incidents. He objects to a play that seems artificial, that does not correspond to life, yet we have said that a truly æsthetic enjoyment demands a sense of unreality. The seeming contradiction is readily explained by the fact that the object may be as real in the sense of true to life, as is consistent with the intent of the artist, but the attitude of the observer should be different from that generally

[1] *Das Wesen der Kunst*, p. 81.

assumed toward the world. If we are able to maintain an æsthetic attitude, the most stirringly real play will continue to be a play for us, and the most ultra-realistic picture will continue to be a work of art, and the most life-like statue will remain for us a series of graceful lines in marble; that is, we shall have maintained our distance, and the object will have remained an object of beauty.

§ 8. THE APPEAL TO OUR PERSONAL DESIRES

If we are to live passively in the object of art, must our own personality be entirely suppressed? Are we to enjoy the unity of plot or the grace of line only in an entirely abstract manner, so distant from the content that we are entirely indifferent to it? Must all art have as formal an appeal as that of most musical compositions or symphonies of color in fine art? Should art have no human appeal? Without further explanation, such conclusions might be drawn from what has been said, but notwithstanding the efforts of some artists and critics, the history of æsthetic appreciation and the evidence of the present day point to the fact that the art if it is to last must be a warm, living art, made for human beings and not intellectual machines, appealing not only through the formal arrangement but through the subject-matter, that is, through the content or meaning of such arrangement.

Every individual has within him the possibility

of definite modes of response which constitute
his personality. In the unconscious, or as some
would say the sub-conscious, are what may be
called suppressed complexes. A complex involves
"wishes" according to Dr. E. B. Holt, who thus
describes the latter term: "This 'wish,' which as a
concept Freud does not analyze, includes all that
would commonly be so classed, and also whatever
would be called impulse, tendency, desire, purpose,
attitude, and the like; not including, however,
any emotional components thereof. . . . An exact
definition of the 'wish' is that it is *a course of action*
which some mechanism of the body is *set* to carry
out, whether it actually does so or does not. . . .
We shall do well if we consider this wish to be,
as in fact it is, dependent on a *motor attitude* of the
physical body, which goes over into overt action
and *conduct* when the wish is carried into execution." [1] Our acts, even those which seem most
trivial, are to some extent controlled by our unconscious desires, hopes and impulses, although we
are for the most part unaware of the true motives.
At times we are dimly conscious of the true reason
for our acts. At other times it may be of such a
nature that we do not care to acknowledge it even
to ourselves. We therefore rationalize our acts,
in our own minds, thus deceiving ourselves, as,
for example, when we refuse to contribute to char-
ity because, as we tell our conscience, we do not

[1] *The Freudian Wish*, pp. 3–4. The mechanism of unconscious tendencies
is explained in the last chapter, entitled "Response and Cognition."

quite approve of some of the methods of the organization, the true reason being, and we are aware
of the fact in the dim recesses of our minds, that
we do not care to spend the money. Now to appeal to such unconscious desires is to gain our interest, and the more fundamental the desire, the
stronger will be the appeal.

It may be objected, however, that the above
facts are in contradiction to the previous statement that we must live in the object of appreciation, allowing ourselves to be passively swayed
hither and thither by it. How can we give ourselves up so completely and still fulfill our own
desires? The answer is to be found in the fact that
the work of art must be of such a nature that we
can find expression for our wishes in it. Not only
should the work of art touch our wishes and in that
way interest us, but it must provide the means for
the complete fulfillment of the wish within the
object itself, if it is to remain art for the observer.
Undoubtedly some of the pleasure in art form is
due to the fact that we can realize in a world of
unreality wishes and impulses that we otherwise
should not desire to express or for whose realization the opportunity would never be offered. The
wish is released and the sense of unreality relieves
us of the necessity of rationalization. The stage
probably makes the strongest appeal to these underlying wishes, and it is here that the mechanism
just described is most readily recognized, but it
applies in greater or less degree to all forms of art,

no matter how formal. Even in the enjoyment of the rhythm of lines unconscious impulses are involved which give meaning to the experience. Art for art's sake, if by the phrase is meant that art should be independent of all content, is an abstract rule that is made impossible by the very nature of mind.

It will now be more clearly understood why such terms as "detachment" and "disinterested contemplation" may be misleading. Far from requiring an inhibition of all play of our personality such as exists in an hypnotic trance, we demand and are able to obtain in art the widest scope for the harmless play of those complex systems of impulses which the psychologists believe to constitute the ego.

§ 9. DEGREES OF PERSONAL APPEAL IN THE ÆSTHETIC ATTITUDE

Furthermore if we believe that art should benefit the individual and improve the race, it should appeal to as many impulses and desires as is consistent with the maintenance of the æsthetic attitude. Dr. Bullough has expressed this idea by saying that we should have as little distance as possible without losing our distance—a rule which he calls "the antinomy of distance." As thus formulated, it would mean literally an infinitesimal amount of distance. Dr. Bullough has unfortunately used the word distance to cover two distinct facts: the amount of appeal which is one of the factors underlying the attitude, and the æsthetic attitude itself. There is a certain advantage in speaking of the varying strength of the appeal to our wishes in terms of distance, but that must not be identified with the essential attitude toward beauty, for we can have more or less distance, but we cannot have degrees of æsthetic attitude. We are either appreciating an object æsthetically or we are not. At any given time, we are either concerned with the beauty of the object or with some other value of the same. Just as soon, for example, as ethical considerations occur to our mind, our attitude shifts. It is not at one and the same time partly ethical and partly æsthetic. On the other hand, there may be so rapid a shifting of the attitude that on reflection our pleasure seems to come from a mixed source. Such a change of interest is comparable to a rapid shift of attention between two activities so that it appears as if we were doing two separate things at the same time, such as listening to two different conversations.

Although it is desirable to have as much human appeal as possible, it is evident that the more appeal there is, other things being equal, that is, the less distance, the more likelihood there will be of loss of æsthetic attitude. That is the danger that is run, and one that those who advocate art for art's sake hesitate to take. The bugle call, for example, sets off too strong a complex, that of hunger and its usual accompaniment in the form of a food-seeking reaction. It is seldom that such a strong biological appeal will be resisted, except perhaps by a musician who is in the act of composing a domestic symphony and whose interest is in expressing the dinner concept by the tone harmonies.

The presence of little distance is the explanation for the general non-æsthetic character of the appeal to our so-called lower senses, for such an appeal is to desires of a strongly personal nature. It is through the appetites that most of our important adjustments to the environment, that is our essential habits, are formed. When, therefore, the appeal to the lower senses is æsthetic, it is because attention has been strongly directed to the relation of such sensory experience to the rest of the art object rather than to ourselves. An example would be a reproduction of the odor of the lemon trees in an Italian scene presented on the stage. The fact that the scene has been laid in a distant and relatively unfamiliar land acts as an aid in maintaining the æsthetic attitude since it presents a setting which has small likelihood of touching off an independent form of response. To those who are familiar with the particular place in question, however, there is here involved the factor already mentioned, that is, appeal to our personal experience, which has a very strong hold upon us both emotionally and in the form of a tendency to action in a definite and individualistic manner. To most individuals a painting of the Hardanger Fjord in Norway would be a work of art under almost all circumstances, but for one who has lived at the particular location represented by the picture, too many specific responses would be involved and there would be interference with the attitude desired by the artist. However, appeal can safely be made to unconscious impulses so long as the art form does not present a situation too familiar to the observer. An abstract idea such as "ambition," notwithstanding the fact that it is one of the strongest forces in society, can safely be the theme of a drama. This is especially true if the situations are not too close to our own time, as for example in the dramatization of scenes from the life of Cæsar or Napoleon. Such scenes will be sufficiently familiar to the average individual to be appreciated and yet will have enough distance to preserve the æsthetic attitude.

Temporal remoteness is a strong factor in preserving the attitude. Pictures, plays, statues, which represent the life of the past generation hold the observer in the land of beauty with little difficulty. It is comparatively easy to keep one's attitude when reading Shakespeare or witnessing his plays, and the same is true of the miracle plays. At the time they were written, however, they appealed much more directly to the everyday life of the people, just as do many of the plays of the present time; consequently they had not the æsthetic effect they have at present. Many pictures and plays of the world war, although intensely interesting, have at present difficulty in

holding us in an æsthetic attitude. Compare the
effect of a very realistic painting of the Battle of
the Marne with the battle scenes by Verestchagin
in the gallery at Moscow. Realistic though the
latter are, and close to our general interests, for
realism was the avowed aim of Verestchagin,[1] yet
they are so far removed both as regards time
and place, that they are relatively easy to enjoy
æsthetically.

The purpose of presenting human motives in
idealized form is evidently to hold the observers
faithful in the path of beauty, and at the same time
to touch their deep-seated wishes. The Greeks
have probably been the most successful in this,
and that is one reason for the strength of the æsthetic appeal of their art. Not only is the intrinsic
value of Greek superior to that of Roman art,
but the latter being more realistic tends to break
down the attitude by its lack of distance.

It is difficult to interest a child in the beauty of
objects if they are similar to its accustomed surroundings, for its interest lies then primarily in
identifying familiar objects, but it is readily understood why this and other biological attitudes
should be uppermost in children and primitive
people who are in the early stages of adjustment to
their environment. It is therefore customary and
advisable, if we desire to direct the child's atten-

[1] Verestchagin's concept of realism is very well brought out in his essay
"Realism," Second Appendix to catalogue of the Verestchagin Exhibition,
1889-1890.

tion to the beauty of things, to present scenes which idealize reality. Very few children will miss the dramatic incidents in the fairy tales. Although they are removed from accustomed experiences, they play upon the strongest human instincts.

An interesting effect of distance is observed in the reaction to the comic. In order that the comic may appear amusing, it must touch off some strong complex in the individual and offer a vehicle for its release. In order that this release may appear pleasant and amusing, great distance is effected through the technique of the comic, which gives the wish an apparently harmless aspect. Frequently the appeal appears very abstract though in reality it is a fundamental one. Indeed, the distance is often so well achieved through the clever mechanism that the pleasure appears to be entirely in the dramatic aspect of the joke. It is by reason of the attitude of detachment thus produced that jokes of somewhat suggestive content are sometimes countenanced for the moment although they may distress one on further reflection.

If art is too far idealized and too distant in its appeal, its influence will be limited. If it has too little distance, that is if it deals with incidents of the present day and of local interest, it is likely to lose its art character, so that we have here two horns of a dilemma. The playwright with high ideals of his art shudders at the thought of catering to the wishes of the modern audience. The mere

suggestion of the white lights of Broadway chills
his blood. Therefore, he writes his play regardless
of the pulse of the time. Critics praise it, drama
leagues recommend it, but the playhouse remains
half empty, for the reason that it is too formal.
It is necessary to meet the existing thoughts and
desires at least halfway, even if for a time the
æsthetic appeal is lessened, provided that the content or meaning does not predominate to such an
extent that the artistic form is quite unperceived.
There is little value in an art that is doomed to
empty galleries and halls. Even the plays of
Shakespeare at the present time have not the hold
upon the people that their artistic merit deserves,
and this is due both to their too great distance, and
to the ignorance on the part of the public of the
formal aspects of art.

The experienced art lover is able to keep his
attitude under almost any circumstances. It
little matters how replete with personal meaning
the picture, play, or statue may be, he can respond to its intrinsic beauty, because he is able to
perceive and appreciate all the deep subtleties of
the formal elements which, through their abstract
nature, touch off only general tendencies and modes
of action.

It is not necessary to restrict art to the formal
appeal, but it is essential to the maintenance of
the æsthetic attitude that a knowledge of the formal
elements should become part of our intellectual
background, so that these elements will be an

effective factor in our æsthetic reactions. It is not meant by this that we consciously isolate the formal elements and pass judgment upon them while enjoying a work of art æsthetically. When we become intellectually occupied in coldly estimating the merits of the lines of a statue, or the dramatic construction of a play, we slip from the attitude of æsthetic enjoyment to the attitude of the critic. In the former attitude we respond emotionally to a situation of which the lines and forces that we have learned to perceive through experience and education form an integral part. The æsthetic attitude may follow as the result of a critical attitude, but it is not identical with it.

So long as the formal elements, the modes of presentation, are fully appreciated, the story or content can be as close to one's every interest as is consistent with the purpose of the artist. Students of literature who visit a melodrama of the old type are able to enjoy its Elizabethan form of construction even though the subject may be that of a celebrated murder. In short, it is by increasing our knowledge of the formal elements of art that we find our solution for the dilemma.

The strength of the formal appeal depends upon both the talent of the artist and the experience of the appreciator. By reason of the cleverness of his technique, the master may with impunity present content of little distance and the appreciator or connoisseur by reason of his knowledge of the formal elements maintains his attitude no matter how much there is of content, or how close it may be. It follows that the public should be educated to observe the relations in art. It should know the value of lines and colors and the laws of the drama. It should be trained to distinguish the pitch of tones and the various overtones; to recognize the musical intervals, the "feel" of lines, the pose of statues and the conflict of forces, and the many other elements which are included under the term formal. Courses in the history of art should lay emphasis upon the development of this side of art, provided it is made clear that this is only one element in appreciation. If that is done artists need be less concerned about the attitude of their public. Their works will be judged according to their purely æsthetic value and the enjoyment will be conditioned by a response of the entire organism.

A certain balance depending upon circumstances must therefore be maintained between the two sources of the appeal, that of the form and that of the content. Unless the formal is made prominent the art will not stand much content, and conversely, if there is little content, there will be a limited field of æsthetic influence unless the form is made sufficiently evident, as is the case in decorative designs and music which depend almost entirely upon their formal appeal.

In the explanation of the depth of the appeal, one may find the reason why certain works of art endure and others disappear. In the complex of

impulses that make up the personality it can be
assumed that some are more fundamental than
others. There are the desires and wishes of the
moment, purely local and individual; beyond these
are others of a more general character belonging
to the inhabitants of a district; then come those
peculiar to the race; and finally those which are
the foundation of human character.[1] It is these
last that the great and enduring masterpieces
touch, and the greater the art, the more completely are these impulses involved. The works
of such artists as Homer, Praxiteles, Da Vinci,
Shakespeare occur to one. They are the creation
of men who are above nationality and who are
claimed by all countries. Even during the World
War, when passions ran high and alien products
were barred, it seemed absurd not to present the
classical works of the enemy in music and drama,
for they are the products and property of the human race. It is the depth of the appeal to deep-
lying, fundamental reactions of the race which has
caused the simple folk-lore and folk music to endure, and it is the same factor which has preserved certain compositions which technically are
inferior art.

In industrial art, the very fact that the object
has a twofold purpose makes it more difficult at

[1] H. Taine in his essay "On the Ideal in Art" (*Lectures on Art*, vol. I., pp.
210–226, translated by John Durand) describes "the various layers of ideas
and sentiments" in man. These are, 1st "the grafted manners" which
last a few years; 2d, the ideas of a generation; 3d those of an historic
period like the Middle Ages; 4th, "the primitive substratum."

times to view the products as things of beauty, than in the case of other forms of artistic expression. Just as, however, a word if repeated a sufficient number of times loses its meaning and becomes, as it were, "hollow sound," so in regard to household utensils, after we have become accustomed to them, they may lose for us much of their meaning and appear merely as objects of shape and color. There is another factor that influences the æsthetic judgment of some persons during the early period of acquisition, namely, that their pleasure is very much determined by the fact of possession, by the price, etc.—attitudes certainly opposed to the æsthetic, and it often takes considerable time for these considerations to disappear from their mind. At first, they are uncertain whether they like the object æsthetically or not. It is very difficult to get in the proper frame of mind for such judgment. After several days' acquaintance with such an object, however, we suddenly see it clearly: it is as if a veil had fallen from our eyes, and we know positively whether we like it or not. It has taken time to complete the adjustment from one attitude to the other, and to make a sufficiently true æsthetic analysis for a clear decision. In the appreciation of domestic architecture this is particularly noticeable. From the architect's sketch we can estimate the artistic effect of a house, but during construction and immediately after completion, we are so occupied with our adjustment to it as a place of abode, that it is sometimes impossible to form an opinion as to its beauty. In that case it is only after some weeks or months that we feel certain that our perception of line is sufficiently abstract to be a reliable basis for a truly æsthetic reaction. Indeed, sometimes we realize as in a flash and with a feeling of surprise that the house is not entirely pleasing. Finally, it may be said that a lapse of time is often necessary also in regard to objects which are primarily works of art, such as pictures and sculpture, especially when the idea of rarity and sense of possession are prominent.

CHAPTER IV

THE ÆSTHETIC ATTITUDE (*Continued*)

§ 1. AIDS FOR THE ÆSTHETIC ATTITUDE IN THE VARIOUS ARTS

IN the preceding chapter we considered for the most part the mental factors in the æsthetic attitude. It remains to enumerate some of the characteristics of the objects which influence this attitude, and especially their bearing upon distance. The first question is concerned with the relative strength of the appeal of the various arts. Toward which form of beauty do we have the least distance? It will probably be agreed that music being, as has been stated, the most formal of the arts, induces the greatest distance on the part of the audience, and that the drama creates the least distance, but the ranking of the other arts is open to criticism. A tentative arrangement would be, ranking from most to least distance: music, literature, fine arts, sculpture, architecture, drama, including dancing. Such a scheme has not very much importance, however, for so much depends upon the various factors within the art itself. For example, highly idealized drama may have much more distance-producing effect under certain conditions, than certain musical compositions of the

modern school. It is, indeed, less profitable to
discuss the relative distance values of the various
arts than to examine those factors within the art
which produce and those which reduce the human
appeal.

A familiar experience is that of the loss of distance which occurs in witnessing a production by a
stock company. After we have seen several plays
by the same company we become familiar with the
personality of the actors apart from the particular
rôle they may be taking. There is then aroused in
us a conflict between his part in the play and our
idea of the actor as an individual, independent of
the requirements of the plot. This latter conception takes us frequently beyond the frame of the
drama. The actor stands out in the picture as a
man we know.

A. *In Music*

So long as music remains strictly formal, it
induces extreme distance. With the introduction
of a "program," it becomes more difficult to hold
an æsthetic attitude, and it is for that reason that
"program" music is often decried. Attempts have
been made to add content to music by the simul-
taneous presentation of illustrations, as for example the flashing on the screen of pictures by
Nicolas Poussin, accompanied by music representative of that artist's moods. A certain success
may be achieved by such methods, but they are
usually condemned by music lovers, who are pro-

verbially most jealous guardians of the distance
of their favorite form of art.

Although music needs few artificial factors for
enhancing distance, yet greater effect is obtained
when an orchestra is enclosed in the frame of the
stage and raised slightly from the floor, thus separating it somewhat from the audience. The difference is slight, but nevertheless real and can be
readily realized by comparing the effect of a
drawing-room recital with that of the concert
hall. The change is due not alone to the fact that
the effect of sound is different when heard at a
greater distance or under better acoustical conditions, there is also a subtle difference in the quality
of our attitude.

B. *In Architecture*

The ordinary observer of architecture is primarily interested in it as a place in which to live.
The more this purpose is concealed, the greater the
distance produced. When the mass and lines are
made prominent it is relatively easy for most to
consider it from the viewpoint of beauty. The
effect of the buildings of New York City from the
Harbor or of some of the modern seaside hotels il-
lustrates this point. It has been a canon of architecture that buildings should honestly represent the use for which they were constructed. In
order to do this and yet to restrain its assertiveness
as a dwelling, many architects strive to make their
houses as low as possible. They thus produce the

effect of their having sprung from the soil with the trees and foliage. Another obvious reason for this tendency, as will be seen later, is in order to produce a unity between the dwelling and the landscape. The triumphal arch is a very good example of a form of architecture which has been taken out of its natural setting. Its original purpose as a gateway is less apparent and it is by most judged and frequently condemned on purely æsthetic grounds.

C. *In Sculpture*

Sculpture in representing lifelike figures in three dimensional forms sets off the anti-æsthetic tendency. Much has therefore been done to increase its distance. It would be difficult to view æsthetically a statue which was in natural colors and in modern costume, and which stood with feet firmly planted on the floor and in the act of walking. Upon a certain well-constructed mountain road there is the statue of the civil engineer, life size, with frock coat and top hat, about to step off a rock. It is almost impossible to see in this anything but the grotesque. The cast iron dogs and other objects which sometimes adorn the lawns of the newly rich are very obvious examples of the disturbing effect of lack of distance, and this is apart from the pain caused by total absence of artistic value. As soon as statues are placed upon pedestals, they are separated from their surroundings, and distance is increased. It does not seem

advisable to use colors, especially if the statues
are very realistic. It is true that although the
archaic statues of the Greeks are tinted, yet it is
very easy for us to see their beauty, nor is there a
tendency to shift our attitude. It must be remembered, however, that in the first place, the
figures are idealized, and secondly the factor of
time strongly influences the setting, and thirdly
the formal side is superbly represented and holds
the attention. On the other hand, what the effect
was on the Greeks at that time is a matter of con-
jecture. As has been stated above, the æsthetic
attitude tends to break down before the Roman
statues which are more realistic, nearer in time
and inferior in line to the Greek statues. It requires a very good statue indeed to hold the entire
æsthetic interest if it is colored. Sculptors have
almost always avoided clothing their figures in
the style of the times. It is not merely for the
sake of dignity that figures of public men are so
frequently clothed in the toga. The costume is a
compromise between the nude and the more
modern clothes. Even though the statue is in
white marble and upon a pedestal, if it represents,
let us say, a recently departed queen dressed in the
habit of the day, including lace parasol and be-
feathered hat, there is a very decided jar to our
æsthetic sense as we come upon it in the midst of
the flowers and trees of Her Majesty's garden. If
it were life size, the shock would be greater than
if conspicuously larger or smaller. Further, the

railings around public statues and the fences about houses not only protect the statues and houses from material injury, but also act to some extent, as a distance-enhancing factor.

In sculpture as soon as more than one figure is introduced, the distance is greatly decreased, due to the added content. There is a tendency to avoid numerous figures except in reliefs, where the effect of the third dimension is lessened. Also, suggested movement within the group is kept at a minimum when the æsthetic effect is carefully considered. In Egyptian art, the figures are represented in conventional and artificial attitudes which, together with the formal treatment of the figures as a whole, inspires great distance in the modern spectator, and must at the time have increased the desired religious effect by inhibiting to some extent mundane thoughts.

D. *In Fine Arts*

When we turn from sculpture to pictures, we leave the world of three dimensions for that of flat surfaces. No matter how realistically the painter may represent the third dimension in his pictures, we are nevertheless adjusted to a flat surface so far as our visual apparatus is concerned, and that.in itself is a very strong factor in distance, and one which permits the safe employment of many more realistic touches than the sculptor would care to risk. Color is here in place. The nature of the costume makes relatively little difference, and many more details may be included in the incidents portrayed. That does not mean, however, that the degree to which the space is represented does not affect one's attitude in admiring pictures. In this regard there is a noticeably different effect between one's attitude before a picture of Van Eyck where space is flattened out, and before a painting at the height of the Renaissance where the eye travels down long vistas of space. The frame is almost essential to the picture, and after what has been said, it is not necessary to enlarge upon its functions. It is one of the less subtle though usual methods of distancing the object, and is therefore most frequently used as an illustration of what is meant by isolating a work of art.[1]

The result of accentuating those features of a picture which have the strongest human appeal and removing the isolating influences of the frame may be seen in the Wiertz Museum in Brussels,

[1] In Mr. Arthur Symons' book *Studies in Seven Arts*, p. 141, we find Whistler's opinion of the value of the frame. "It was one of Whistler's aims in portrait-painting to establish a reasonable balance between the man as he sits in the chair, and the image of the man reflected back to you from the canvas. 'The one aim,' he wrote, 'of the unsuspecting painter is to make his man "stand out" from the frame—never doubting that, on the contrary, he should, and in truth absolutely does, stand *within* the frame—and at a depth behind it equal to the distance at which the painter sees his model. The frame is, indeed, the window through which the painter looks at his model, and nothing could be more offensively inartistic than this brutal attempt to thrust the model on the hither-side of this window!' Here, as always, it was the just limit of things which Whistler perceived and respected. He never proposed, in a picture, to give you something which you could mistake for reality; but frankly, a picture, a thing which was emphatically not nature, because it was art."

where some of the paintings, as realistic as the talent of the artist could make them, are viewed through a small opening in a screen surrounding the picture, thus increasing the naturalness through the appearance of greater depth. The intention here, however, seems evidently to have been to startle rather than to please æsthetically.

No serious artist would think of allowing his figures to break the line of the frame, for he knows that in so doing he will influence the attitude of his public as well as that of himself. A good example of such an effect, where in fact everything is done to decrease distance, is to be found in the modern panorama where real guns, wheels, wagons, and human figures are placed in the foreground in front of the canvas. This together with the enormous size of the canvas, which almost precludes the possibility of unifying the scene, not to mention the frequent lack of artistic talent displayed, makes an appraisal from the standpoint of beauty, practically impossible for most observers. It is indeed the work of the craftsman rather than the artist. Even such a trivial thing as the embossing of the gold on canvasses such as those of Crevelli, or the insertion of bits of colored glass or jewels, unless they are seen at a great distance, interfere with one's mood by too realistically suggesting actual objects in all three dimensions. The strong distance-producing effect of a two dimensional representation of three dimensional form may be further noticed in regard to the motion picture.

The factor of motion and the photographic representation would be hard to respond to other than non-æsthetically, especially as the formal elements so frequently have little artistic value, if it were not that the scene is unfolded on a plane surface. This fact, together with the unaccustomed and unconscious set of the organism in fusing the rapidly succeeding pictures into the perception of movement, aids one in maintaining, at least at times, an æsthetically critical attitude toward the play. If other things were equal, that is, if the formal side and the nature of the content were the same in the photoplay and in the legitimate drama, it would follow, from what has just been stated, that the æsthetic attitude would be more readily maintained before the photoplay. Most of us have probably experienced this at times.[1]

E. *In the Drama and Literature*

The proscenium frame acts in the same way for the play as does the frame for the picture, and just as it decreases the distance to have an encroachment upon the outline of the frame, in the same, if not in greater degree, is the æsthetic effect spoiled when a bridge or runway is built between the stage and the rear of the orchestra seats to enable actresses to walk over the shoulders of the audience.[2]

[1] Münsterberg has described several factors of distance (*Principles of Art Education*, pp. 37–40).

[2] Some of the modern methods of obtaining distance in stage scenery are described in Oliver M. Sayler's *The Russian Theatre Under the Revolution*.

In regard to the scenic effect, the critics of the drama differ widely. The peculiar beauty of a Shakespeare play, when given with the meagre scenery of the Elizabethan drama, is of course due in part to the distance lent by the stage arrangements. Realistic scenery, on the other hand, has its advantages, but it requires a very cleverly developed technique and a theme of fundamental importance if the play is to remain an æsthetic object rather than a bit of real life. The present tendency in the direction of simplified and suggestive, rather than realistic, setting has done much to enhance the beauty of the play, and to hold the æsthetic attention of the audience. For example, in Mr. Gordon Craig's setting for a forest in the play of Hamlet there are none of the usual details of moss-covered rocks, twisted roots and scattered bushes—nothing but the tall, gaunt forms of the trees, grouped as masses of dark, oppressive shadows that almost hide the moonlight beyond and cast a spell of deep mystery on the scene.[1] In this way, a strong stimulus is given

On pages 40 and 41 we find "If you are a very naïve and proper playgoer you will still feel only subconsciously the distance of the scene, its air of half-reality; and you will not think to inquire of the surrounding circumstances how this result is attained. But if you are as keenly interested in how things are done in the theatre as you are in what is done, you will see now in the full, but not too full light of the scene that it is all being played at least twenty-five feet back of the curtain line and in addition behind a fine meshed gauze screen. Only dimly can you see the curtains that lead back to this illuminated part of the stage, for the light is so admirably controlled that the intervening distance is potent but not obtrusive."

[1] The illustration, which is for Act I, scene 4, of *Hamlet*, is in E. G. Craig's *On the Art of the Theatre*, p. 136.

to the imagination, which is an important function
in the enjoyment of beauty, but there is little to
excite those impulses which are opposed to the
unity of the play. Such treatment, by its general
nature, apart from any particular merit, is almost
unanimously judged to be artistic.

When the play itself has much distance, as in Mr.
Granville Barker's production of Anatole France's
The Dumb Wife, the æsthetic effect of the highly
idealized and formal settings is readily obtained.
The distance is very great, yet the appeal of the
beauty of construction is so evident that the bond
between play and audience is maintained with
ease. The highly conventionalized and fantastic
settings and costumes of Bakst, with their unusual play of strong colors and sharply contrasting
lines, have considerable distance value, not only
because of the departure from realism but also on
account of the boldness with which the formal
elements of the scene are presented and forced
upon the audience. The Urban scenery has frequently a similar effect. Even where the scenes
are realistically represented the distance is preserved through the strength of color combinations
and the artistic arrangement of lines.

When dancing is presented within the frame of
the stage it becomes more readily a unified series
of graceful movements and less a conscious re-
minder of personal experience, and it is still farther
removed when the postures are conventionalized
like those seen in early Egyptian sculpture or

when the movements are timed to express the *motifs* of classical music as in the dancing of the Duncan School.

In literature, there is merely the symbol to represent the object, so that there is little direct appeal to the senses so far as the content is concerned. On the other hand, it is a stronger stimulus for thought and although it is comparatively easy to remain absorbed in the story, æsthetic enjoyment is likely to be derived by the general reader more from the factors of suspense and release than from any other intrinsic merits of the literary form as such. Poetry has the advantage of prose in its formal appeal and consequently in the distance induced in the reader. The value of this for the æsthetic effect has been so clearly recognized that those modern writers who are in revolt against conventional forms of poetry have cast prose in a form which brings out the sound and rhythm values; at the same time, through the content they call up colors and shapes of visual perception, thus combining with the factors peculiar to literature, those of fine arts and music.

§ 2. Relation of Beauty to Truth

From what has been said regarding the attitude it is possible to separate ethical considerations from those of æsthetics. There are several questions involved. In the first place, must art represent the truth or may it under certain conditions deceive? Secondly, should art be moral,

and lastly, should art point a moral? Regarding
the first, Ruskin has taken a very strong stand in
the "Lamp of Truth." [1] He says that when in
architecture there is deliberate deception the pro-
cedure must be condemned. When, however, there
is no chance of our accepting the representation
as genuine, when there is every evidence that it
is an imitation, then the method is legitimate.
The fan tracery on the roof of the Milan Cathedral
is so realistically done and so far aloft that it
easily deceives. "This is, of course, gross degrada-
tion." On the other hand, on the roof of the
Sistine Chapel there are architectural designs in
grissaille which blend beautifully with the frescoes. The unity is perfect and as the frescoes are
known to be paintings, the grissaille work is also
perceived as such. There is therefore no deception and the form of decoration is permissible. A
similar comparison is made between the plaster
of the façades of the houses of Venice and Verona,
which is decorated with frescoes and the cement
which covers brick and is marked off to represent
blocks of stone.[2] The granite foundation of the
staircase of the British Museum is "mocked at its
landing by an imitation, the more blamable because tolerably successful. The only effect of it is
to cast a suspicion upon the true stones below, and
upon every bit of granite afterward encountered.
One feels a doubt, after it, of the honesty of Memnon

---

[1] *Seven Lamps of Architecture.*
[2] *Ibid.,* Illustrated Library Edition, Colonial Press Company, pp. 48–49.

himself." [1] Veneer such as that used in San Marco in Venice, even though it is of the most glorious color, is deprecated. According to Ruskin, it is as reprehensible for an architect to use imitation decorations as for a woman to wear false jewelry.

These and the many other illustrations give excellent examples of a certain confusion of issue which frequently occurs. There is first the mere fact of deception as such, judged according to ethical values, and secondly the skill of the deception, and thirdly the effect of the knowledge of the nature of the deceiving material upon the total harmony. If an imitation is carried out so cleverly that one cannot detect it, unless one is told, then the displeasure due to the deception is the result of an ethical and not an æsthetic attitude. It is then every individual's choice to assume such an ethical attitude, but it will undoubtedly interfere with the sense of beauty. In fact, it will probably inhibit any æsthetic reaction, and it should be recognized that the judgment then is not upon the intrinsic artistic merit of the object. It should, however, in the case of a clever imitation be quite possible to abstract from any such ethical considerations and view the object entirely from the standpoint of a work of art. Ruskin in writing upon the substitution of cast or machine work for hand wrought decoration, remarks: "There are two reasons, both weighty, against this practice; one, that all cast and ma-

[1] *Op. cit.*, p. 51.

chine work is bad, as work; the other, that it is dishonest. Of its badness, I shall speak in another place, that being evidently no efficient reason against its use when other cannot be had. Its dishonesty, however, which, to my mind, is of the grossest kind, is, I think, a sufficient reason to determine absolute and unconditional rejection of it." [1] According to the distinction just made between the attitudes, the rejection on account of its badness is founded upon artistic merit, and that upon its dishonesty upon considerations other than those of beauty.

In regard to the wearing of false jewels, it is obvious that the total pleasure is greater when the jewels are genuine, for there are very few who are not to a slight extent influenced by the monetary value. If, however, one is entirely concerned with their decorative value, if the pleasure is due to the color, shape, luster, etc., then it is the beauty alone that counts. The attitude is strictly æsthetic and it is a matter of indifference that they are imitations. In fact, it may be that the imitations are more beautiful and are therefore preferred. The same remarks apply to antique furniture. In collecting such objects, most of us prefer originals. It is evident, however, that the interest is too often upon that characteristic alone. It is rarity that is of first importance and not beauty, for everything is collected, from truly beautiful old pieces of furniture to tin pans and door knobs, simply

[1] *Op. cit.*, p. 55.

because it is old. The idea of deception must be prominent in the mind when such a motive is back of the desire, and is a witness to the non-æsthetic set of the individual, although it must be admitted that there are many who have running parallel to this desire for originals, but not identical with it, a strongly developed sense of beauty which, however, is too frequently pushed farther and farther into the background of consciousness with the growth of the collecting mania.

In the presence of old things, it is very difficult, even though we are desirous of giving a judgment strictly upon the beauty of the object, not to allow rarity to influence us. Miss Kate Gordon has made an interesting experiment upon the judgment of the beauty of antique rugs. They were shown to a number of people including a few experts. That the experts should differ from the others was to be expected. Several of them, however, confessed that the rarity had been an unavoidable factor in the choice. To take another example from rugs, there are two distinct designs of the Kulah rug, one with parallel stripes in the border, the other with a more complicated design. The latter design is less common and when one has searched for years for an example it is beyond human power to inhibit a mingling of the joy of the discovery with the pleasure in its intrinsic beauty.

The desire for collecting becomes a fetish which kills every other impulse. It is rarely that one elicits a sympathetic response from the collector of coins if one calls his attention to the beauty of the design of one of his less valuable pieces. He will probably reply, with some show of impatience, that it has artistic merit, but that he wants to show you a very old coin that he has. When one is buying furniture honestly for its decorative effect, if the price is merely what one would have to pay for an imitation, then the question whether or not it is an original should not occur. We presuppose, of course, that one knows beauty when one sees it. Most imitations are less beautiful, however, than originals, because they are poor imitations, so that ordinarily one feels safer in accepting genuineness as an indirect criterion rather than to rely upon one's direct perception and power of analysis. In short, it can be stated that if objects such as old furniture are imitated so well that one cannot tell the difference, the æsthetic appreciation of the imitation should be as high as that of the original, and it should be recognized if one desires to be entirely honest with oneself, that any other judgment is influenced by commercial value, question of ethics, or degree of antiquity.

To return for a moment to what Ruskin terms "surface deceits," that is the use of plaster for stone, veneer for solid marble, etc., there is a consideration which is an æsthetic one but it is entirely apart from any idea of deception as such. Ordinarily it should make no difference in the actual beauty whether the columns in St. Isaacs in Petrograd are of solid lapis lazuli or not, or whether the marble forming the walls of the palace ball room in Budapest is real marble or only painting on plaster. When, however, one happens to know that plaster is used instead of a more solid material, one feels an uneasiness from one's knowledge of the nature of the substituted material, lest there be not sufficient strength to oppose the downward pull of gravity. Architects with a highly developed sense of beauty, lament the use of composition slabs for marble. Unconsciously the weakness of the material influences their total set toward the building, even though they are aware that the structure is sufficiently well supported by steel girders. The ideas associated by experience with composition are sufficient to change one's adjustments, even though one is aware of counteracting influences. Psychology has shown that our perception is constantly influenced by such subconscious or semiconscious factors. This is readily observed in the effect of size on the weight of an object. Even though we may know that the two objects are of equal weight, yet if they are of unequal size, the larger will seem the lighter. A pound of feathers actually feels lighter than a pound of lead. If it is such considerations concerning substitutes which affect our judgments, considerations which influence one's perception of those very features of an object which are universally acknowledged to belong to its beauty, such as the dynamic quality of lines in architecture, then the attitude has remained an æsthetic one. If based upon such features of experience, arguments against surface deceit find a legitimate place in treatises on beauty.

§ 3. RELATION OF BEAUTY TO MORALITY

Should ethical principles influence art, and if so, to what extent? There are two extremes which have been reached in this regard. In all ages, there have been those who have tried to place a ban upon anything which seemed risqué or morally unconventional. When such a movement has reached any considerable magnitude, a reaction has set in from the side of the artist. Those who advocate art for art's sake then proclaim that any subject is entirely permissible provided it is artistically portrayed, and they have frequently attempted to carry out this principle. Modern secession galleries, notably in Germany, have contained pictures that have sometimes shocked and more often disgusted the most experienced art critics. Yet even such extremists have stopped short of some subjects. The same may be said of literature and the drama.

The problem can be decided upon purely æsthetic grounds, as the artist desires, and not necessarily from the standpoint of the moralist. If the content makes too strong an appeal to immoral tendencies, then it is reprehensible from the artistic point of view, for it tends to create too little distance and the artist loses his audience. There are some incidents in life which the human race is unanimous in finding repulsive, and these will always be barred from artistic representation. For the rest, much depends upon the set of the mind of the audience and the artistic merit of the work, as has been pointed out at length in regard to the attitude in general. It is impossible to formulate general rules, or to say what may be included and what not, for it depends entirely upon the artist and the audience to which he wishes to appeal. When the artistic value of a work of art is universally recognized as very high, then those who would withdraw it from the public gaze, reveal thereby their own state of mind. To insist upon the draping of Greek statues of the classical period or to forbid the production of certain dramas of acknowledged merit are not so much crimes against art as an insult to the community. On the other hand, it is even more reprehensible to appeal as is frequently done to the baser motives of the human race under the cover of art. Even when the object has some artistic value, it is very probable that the public will not respond as intended to the art form, but rather to the suggestive content. It ceases to be an object of art and there exists then sufficient reason why it should be withdrawn from that particular community. Even the statue of the Venus de Milo or Praxiteles' Hermes would have no place in an environment where it was accepted merely as the representation of a naked human form.

The next question is whether art should teach a moral. It is true that the appreciation of beauty

as such has a moral value. The very nature of the
æsthetic attitude, which induces a pleasure entirely free from self-interest in the narrow sense,
makes it an adjustment of the organism which is
extremely commendable from the standpoint of
ethics. For the time one is free from the struggle
which is made necessary by social conditions and
is enabled to attain a broader and more generous
view of the relation of things.

This is not, however, what is generally meant by
the question. It is put by those who feel that there
should be some explicit utilization of art apart
from the mere arousal of pleasure. In fact, there
are extremists who believe that even the pleasure
factor should be subordinated to the development
of morality, and if it cannot serve that purpose art
should be entirely prohibited. That is a question
for ethics to decide. Æsthetics can merely indicate that as soon as a work of art communicates
nothing but a lesson to the observer, it ceases to
be for him a work of art. It is unnecessary, after
what has been said, to show why the experience
is not an æsthetic one. So far as art is concerned,
there is no reason why there should be a moral
appeal. It seems futile from the standpoint of
æsthetics to ask the purpose of the play or the picture or the tale. Some plays are written without any
idea of communicating ethical principles. Some
of Mr. Bernard Shaw's plays, for example, leave
the audience entirely in the dark as to the solution
of the moral problem unintentionally suggested.

Why should one complain of that and torment
one's mind by searching for an answer which the
author, who has been interested solely in his art,
has considered of negligible importance? Even
when the moral problem has been solved, the
answer may not be satisfactory, but the play can
nevertheless be enjoyed if the distance is maintained. The moral appeal, however, is an extremely strong one. Artists know this and it is
due to this fact that many of them insistently refuse to emphasize the ethical side. For the most
part they assume an attitude of indifference to-
wards it, for they know that if motives other than
the creation of beauty should be in their minds
while they are working, their art is likely to suffer.
There will be less vigor due to a relaxed attention to the true art form, and the result will tend
toward the distressingly sentimental, such as is
found in the paintings of certain English schools
which resemble the Christmas art supplements
of popular journals. One should not generalize,
however, for there are those who can weave the
moral so subtly into their artistic fabric that the
effect is as truly æsthetic as can be desired.[1]

At times the play or tale or painting is deliber-

---

[1] Verestchagin has described his own attitude thus:—"A good deal has
been written about my works: many were the reproaches brought against
my paintings, those treating of religious subjects as well as of military. And
yet they were, all of them, painted without any preconceived idea,—were
painted only because their subjects interested me. The moral in each case
appeared afterwards, coming up of its own account, from the very truth-
fulness of impressions." (*Realism*, pp. 11–12.)

ately constructed for propaganda. The author is willing to sacrifice the artistic to his purpose, and the result should be accepted in the spirit in which it was intended. Art of course suffers a certain loss, but the stage or the art gallery may succeed where the pulpit or the lecture platform has failed, so that the method is to some extent justified. Plays like Brieux's "Damaged Goods" must be accepted, if at all, from the pedagogical view-point. It is useless even to discuss the artistic merit of plays of this sort, where the ethical note is so evidently uppermost, for there is little chance of the audience maintaining any distance toward it. It is even a question whether the attitude of moral evaluation can be held in opposition to the even stronger sexual one. Why the artists deprecate such a use of art is evident; it runs counter to all their aims, and the non-æsthetic motives, on account of their strength, would, if encouraged ever so slightly, quite overlay their art.

The purpose of this discussion has been to make clear the true province of æsthetic criticism. It must not be supposed, however, that art is free from all moral laws. Professor R. B. Perry correctly decided this issue when he wrote, "Art is subject to moral criticism, because morality is nothing more nor less than the law which determines the whole order of interests, within which art and every other good thing is possible. It will scarcely be denied that art is an expression of interest, that both its creation and its enjoyment are

activities, moods, or phases of life; and it follows
that before this specific interest can be safely or
adequately satisfied, it is necessary to fulfil the
general conditions that underlie the satisfaction
of all interest. It is as absurd to speak of art for
art's sake as it is to speak of drinking for drinking's sake, if you mean that this interest is entitled
to entirely free play. Art, like all other interests,
can flourish only in a sound and whole society,
and the law of soundness and wholeness in life is
morality. . . . But," he adds, a few pages beyond, "the moralist is judging art *on moral grounds*.
Hence he does not say, 'I see that your painting
is ugly'; but he does say, 'I see that your painting,
which you esteem beautiful (and I take your word
for it) is *bad*.'" [1]

It has been shown that whether or not there is in
any given situation an experience of beauty and
what the degree of the beauty is, depends upon the
nature of the reaction of the human organism,
or in other words, the attitude of mind toward
an object; and this reaction in turn depends both
upon the state of the organism at the time and the
nature of the object. What is meant by the state
of mind, in an æsthetic situation, and how it constantly changes through the interplay of desires,
wishes, and intentions will now be evident. It
will also be clear that even a slight change in the
arrangement of the object of beauty may funda-

---

[1] *The Moral Economy*, pp. 174–176. See also Marshall's *Pain, Pleasure
and Æsthetics*, p. 139.

mentally affect the adjustment of the organism. The statement will now be understood that beauty is neither totally dependent upon the person who experiences, nor upon the thing experienced; that it is neither subjective nor objective, neither the result of purely intellectual activity, nor a value inherent in the object, but a relation between two variables—the human organism and the object. As such, it is just as real as an experience of color or sound. What has been termed beauty does not exist when there is no organism to experience it, so that the enduring quality of the object is not an essential though desirable characteristic of the work of art. It is now necessary to describe more fully the manner in which the organism reacts in an æsthetic situation, and through its adjustment experiences the pleasure of beauty. This will be the subject of the next chapter.

CHAPTER V

EMPATHY

§ 1. THE MOTOR RESPONSE IN PERCEPTION

IT is not necessary to lift a stone in order to know that it is heavy. The visual perception of the size and nature of the stone is sufficient to arouse within us, through association with previous experiences of lifting, the muscle sensations or motor set which would accompany the actual process of lifting. Without such previous experience, there would be no perception of weight. The word itself would be without meaning. All of our perceptions are dependent upon the motor attitudes that are assumed toward the object. The eye measures the extent of a line by moving over it, or there is an incipient revival within us of the muscular sensations of some other part of the body, such as the hand or the leg; that is, we think of the movement of that member along the line, and thus have the clue to the length of the line. The perception obtained by the roundness of an object or other factors of shape, depends upon similar processes. When we notice the smooth curves of a marble torso, we can probably, if we observe carefully, get a fleeting image of our hands moving in imagination around the figure. Combined with this sense of movement, there will probably be fancied the coldness of the marble and the quality of the touch. The true distance of objects from us, their shape, and the nature of lines are also given in terms of movement. The meaning of facial expression is learned from the movement of one's own face, or a tendency toward such movement as suggested by the lines of the face observed.[1]

When we listen to a song, we have a tendency to move in time to the rhythm, and to repeat the notes with accompanying tension in the throat. In silent reading, the tendency to movement often goes over into actual movement of the lips or muscles of the larynx. The act of unity itself, fundamental to experience, is conceived in motor terms as a bringing of things together. It will rightly be objected that in many instances of perception there is no consciousness of such movement, not even of the faintest tendency toward such imitation of facial expression as that just described. The answer is that these motor sets may be, and in fact most frequently are, subconscious. The object observed, whether through the eye, ear, or another of the senses, arouses the memory of former movements, which are so revived that they form a nervous pattern; that is, the nerve paths going to the necessary muscle groups are opened, and those to opposed muscle groups are closed, and this pattern, which is ready on

---

[1] See the author's "The Judgment of Emotions from Facial Expressions," *Journal of Abnormal Psychology*, August, 1918.

additional stimulation to produce actual movement, is sufficient to give us our perception of
space, weight, form, smoothness, delicacy, and
many of our other experiences. Accordingly one
must for the most part explain this tendency to
movement in physiological rather than psychological terms.

We can readily prove to our satisfaction that
we do assume a motor attitude to the object of our
perception, even though such an attitude is carried
in unconscious terms, by performing a simple experiment. If we look successively at two pictures
which are identical, except that one is reversed
as in a mirror, the difference in the direction of the
lines of the figures will be felt distinctly as a physical jar, such as is produced by a sudden change
in the direction of a voluntary movement. In
this case as in many other actual experiences, the
motor set assumed toward the object is not noticed
until there is some transition to an attitude that
conflicts with the former one. This may also be
readily observed in regard to our motor set toward
the familiar arrangement of objects about us, such
as those of our room. There is a very faint glow
of familiarity about those possessions which we
perceive every day of the year, and this sense of the
accustomed is carried in terms of ease of adjustment through long practice; but let one thing be
removed or disarranged and instantly there is
felt an uneasiness and motor restlessness, as we
should describe it. We feel that there has been a

change even though at times we are unable to
identify it. When motion is suggested to us, the
motor tendency is even more noticeable, as for
example when we are directed to go down the street
one block, turn to the right, then to the left, etc.
There are many who will, in order to understand
and remember the directions, act them out in imagination so vividly that there will be felt in the body
and extremities a tug to the right or the left.
When an actual motion is visually perceived, the
movement is still more vividly felt. In watching
a football game, we suddenly realize that in the
excitement of following our team, we have been
unconsciously pushing against our neighbor on the
bench. The prestidigitator has no difficulty in
directing the attention away from the sleight of
hand by simply pointing toward the innocent
hand with the fingers of the hand which is to do
the palming.

There are two main forms of motor attitude that
may be assumed in regard to an object, one of
which particularly concerns æsthetics, the other
not. The one is an adjustment toward, the other
an adjustment in the object. When one sees a tree
swaying in the sunshine, one can either have the
motor impulse to put out one's hand to stop the
motion, which is in a sense a defensory attitude,
or one may have the impulse to sway with the moving tree and thus to realize the true nature of its
motion. It is this latter form of adjustment that
has been described by Lotze, and it will probably

be recognized from what has gone before that it is such a reaction that is found in æsthetic enjoyment. It will be recalled that two attitudes may be assumed toward the outstretched hand of a statue: either one of grasping the hand, or of feeling the "outstretching" of the hand. It is through this latter attitude, which gives us the feeling of the tension and the weight of the arm, the angle at which it is raised, and the bend at the elbow and wrist, that we can get the true æsthetic effect. We can feel these qualities of form and motion only by carrying out the movements or experiencing somewhere in the organism a tendency to such muscular adjustments and movements. It is only by such a movement within ourselves that we can have the experience of the æsthetic pleasantness or unpleasantness of things.

§ 2. Lipps' Theory of Empathy

This fact of the dynamic quality of perceptions has been described by Lotze [1] and F. T. Vischer [2] and has even appeared earlier in the literature, but the wider application of the principle to æsthetics was made clear by Theodor Lipps. He termed this phenomenon "Einfühlung" (feeling into), a word which had already been casually used by Lotze, and which has been translated by Professor Titchener as "empathy." [3]

[1] A description of Lotze's views is given in the chapter on "Balance and Proportion," pp. 216 *et seq.*

[2] *Das Schöne und die Kunst*, p. 70.

[3] *Experimental Psychology of the Thought Processes*, p. 21.

Lipps has illustrated his meaning by examples from the appreciation of architecture, vases, etc., and has used the principle also as an explanation of optical illusions. In his first description of his theory of empathy he says: "The Doric column rises [literally rears itself up] as does every column. . . . This self-raising of the column is its 'intrinsic activity.' The word activity is used in the fullest sense as exertion, striving, expenditure of energy; at the same time expenditure of energy through which something is achieved. Such activity is not without opposing activity or resistance, which must be overcome. This [resistance] is here occasioned by the weight. . . . But upon our observing the column and seeing it raise itself to a certain height above the ground, this [resistance] does not prevent the force which is directed against the weight from appearing to us as the actual activity; the force and not the weight will in our eyes seem to perform the act with which we are here concerned or through which the column appears to gain its peculiar property." [1] The manner in which this dynamic quality of inanimate objects is apprehended is explained by Lipps as follows: "A similar way of considering things can be noticed whenever we speak of a 'force' residing in an object; more clearly even whenever we realize a 'tendency' or 'striving' in anything that

[1] *Raumæsthetik und Geometrisch-Optische Täuschungen*, pp. 3–4. Vernon Lee and C. Anstruther-Thomson published a similar theory under the title of "Beauty and Ugliness" in the *Contemporary Review*, Oct. and Nov., 1897.

happens, whenever we realize any 'doing' or 'being done to,' any 'activity' or 'passivity.' All such vivifying of our surrounding realities comes about, and can come about only as we attribute to outer things our own feeling of force, our own feeling of striving or willing, our own activity and passivity. . . . The column seems to brace itself and raise itself, that is to say, to proceed in the way in which I do when I pull myself together and raise myself, or remain thus tense and erect, in opposition to the natural inertness of my body. It is impossible for me to be aware of the column without this activity seeming to exist directly in the column of which I am aware." [1] That is, when we see an object such as a column or a spiral or an arch, we realize from our previous experience how it was constructed. We have an idea of the forces, tensions, etc., involved. There are then induced in our muscles and joints sensations of strain and movement similar to those which we should have if we built such objects. The ideas of these sensations are then projected into the object and these give it life. They are no longer our own sensations but attributes of the object. It is not a mere perception of the form which directly calls up ideas of one's activity and which in turn is projected into the object; for Lipps it is first necessary that we have this knowledge of the process of construction, before we can have the ideas of movement. The perception of

[1] *Op. cit.*, pp. 6-7.

movement, however, is first identified in the object and not in one's self. There is the immediate perception of the rearing of a column, the span of the arch, the motion of the spiral. "Briefly, in the act of empathy I do not supply any form to the spiral or to the manner in which it seems to have been constructed, but it is the forces through which its form has originated to which I attach this personal quality. Nor is it at all necessary that I should have ever realized this form within myself. Inasmuch as this personal quality is added to the form of this definite mechanical process or is incorporated in it, this quality naturally appears as a quality of a mechanical process which is spatially so constituted as to form a spiral." [1] This is the essence of Lipps' theory. He has enlarged upon it in his subsequent writings,[2] but has become more metaphysical in his amplifications, especially in his insistence upon the idea that the projection of our movements is a projection of our ego into the object. Lipps has insisted that there is not in us the actual sensation of muscular effort. He believes in a purely mental process without any sensational basis, an idea which is entirely free from actual experiences of bodily processes, a mystical mind substance, and it is the ideas of movement within us in this, as he would perhaps say, "spiritual sense" that give the inanimate

---

[1] "Æsthetische Einfühlung," *Zeitschrift für Psych. u. Phys. der Sinnesorgane*, vol. 22, 1900, pp. 439–440.

[2] See *Zur Einfühlung*.

objects dynamic force and cause us to realize their true form and shape.

§ 3. MOVEMENTS AND TENDENCIES TO MOVEMENTS

Professor Karl Groos among others, called attention, on the other hand, to the fact that there are often actual sensations of movements of the organism when perceiving shapes, etc. He called his theory "inner mimicry," [1] and as it was contrary to Lipps' spiritual theory, it was bitterly opposed by the latter. The majority of modern experimental psychologists, however, agree with the contentions of Professor Groos. In fact, such actual movements can be detected in the laboratory during experiments upon perception. Lipps, however, is correct in so far that during æsthetic contemplation such experiences are not felt as sensations within the body. In fact, they do not come to consciousness as sensations of our own movements at all, but influence the perception in such a way that the lines and figures themselves seem to have the force which is actually in us. As soon as we are conscious of our own sensations, we are no longer contemplating the beauty of the object, for the words "our own sensations" in themselves denote that we are no longer enjoying the object, but that our æsthetic attitude has broken down under the distraction of the bodily processes. Indeed, as soon as our attention is upon such processes, there can be no identification of such move-

[1] See *Die Spiele des Menschen.*

ments with the lines, no fusion of the sensations with the object, and so even empathy itself is impossible. This fact suggests a further reason why it is so difficult to assume an æsthetic attitude toward objects which are perceived through the lower senses. When one chews and swallows, the sensations from the muscles of the jaw and throat are relatively strong and come readily into consciousness. The same is true of the sensations from the muscles of the nose in smelling, especially when we are interested in the quality of the odor, that is when we sniff carefully. In obtaining touch and temperature stimulations there are also strong sensations from the various muscles of the body, for they are generally moved during the perception. The attention then is partly at least upon the process; things *taste* good, *smell* good, *feel* good. On the other hand, it is seldom that one feels the tension in the eyes or the ears, and so the color *is* pretty, the sound *is* agreeable, etc.[1] The fact that there are sensations of bodily movements or tendencies toward such movements is not learned directly at the time of the spontaneous æsthetic experience, but only when one is definitely set for analytical introspection or else through objective records obtained under experimental conditions.

---

[1] It is probably this projection of our feeling into the object which is the basis of Professor Santayana's definition of beauty as "pleasure objectified." *The Sense of Beauty*, p. 52. See also James' *Essays in Radical Empiricism*, pp. 143–144.

In discussing the possibility of the accompaniment of eye movements in certain perceptions of form, Vernon Lee writes: "This phenomenon is *hidden*, can be watched only in especial experiments like those made by my collaborator as the result of specially trained attention, and is, by the very fact of normal æsthetic attention being withdrawn from the perceiving subject and fixed upon the perceived object, translated at once into qualities of the visible shape (*Beauty and Ugliness*, p. 546). 'Our attention has become engaged, not with the change in ourselves productive of the sense of height, or roundness, or symmetry, but with the objective external causes of these changes; and the formula of perception has become, not 'I *feel* roundness, or height, or symmetry,' but 'this or that object *is* round, or high, or symmetrical.'" [1]

When her collaborator, Miss C. Anstruther-Thomson, made the observations upon which to base the following description, she was for the most part a psychologist and not an æsthetician: "My eye falls on the Venus of Milo. . . . The pressure of my feet on the ground is pressure that I see in a marked degree in the feet of the statue. The lift-up of my body I see done more strongly and amply in her marble body, and the steadying pressure of my head I see in a diminished degree in the poise of the statue's beautiful head. These movements I may be said to imitate, but I should find them

[1] *Beauty and Ugliness*, p. 135.

and imitate them equally in a Renaissance monument or a mediæval chalice. They are at the basis of all art. Another connexion that I feel with her is by the balance and shifting of my weight from side to side in order to follow her balance." [1] The analysis of our motor attitude, however, increases such participation in future æsthetic situations, and these add to the depth and richness of our immediate experience, sharpen the critical function, and heighten the power of discrimination.

Professor Groos believes that there are three different stages in our empathic response. When the bodily feelings, etc., are not perceived as localized in the body, they seem to fill the object; when these sensations are still too weak to induce our attention to wander from the object, but are sufficiently strong to have a decided effect on consciousness, there is a projection of ourselves in the object; if they are still stronger, they will be definitely realized and then there is no longer this projection. [2] The first and last stages are in agreement with what has been said above, and the description is important for an adequate knowledge of the nature of empathy and its relation to the immediate æsthetic appreciation. The existence of a second stage, that of the consciousness of the "projection of ourselves," just as that of Lipps' "projection of the ego," is doubtful. It seems to be a theoret-

[1] *Op. cit.*, p. 119.
[2] "Das Æsthetische Miterleben," *Zeitschrift für Æsthetik*, etc., Vol. IV, part 2, p. 181.

ical assumption and not a fact discernible in experience. If we are conscious of such projection then we are also aware of ourselves; that is, that the sensations are our own sensations, and that therefore they cannot be located in the object, which is what such projection implies. The object seems to have force, to live; that is a fact of experience. It is discovered that such a perception is due to one's own muscle sensations, although at the time of the perception they seem to be a quality of the object. This latter is also a fact of experience. These two facts are empirical and important. It is then, however, assumed that because these muscle sensations condition the quality of the object, there must be some awareness at times of the fact of the projection itself, which is not necessarily true, and is not borne out by experience. In other words, the idea seems to be a logical assumption and not an empirical fact. It has seemed necessary to discuss this point at some length, because it is typical of descriptions which so frequently occur in æsthetic literature, and which in the case of empathy have tended to express in metaphysical terms a perfectly honest and clean-cut experience.

The phenomenon of empathy is not so complicated as one is led to suppose from descriptions like that by Lipps. When we see a form such as a spiral, memories of movements corresponding to the spiral are touched off, probably memories of the movements of the hand in drawing such a figure. If it is an unknown shape, one first seeks the experience of actually tracing the form in order to perceive its quality. These memories are expressed either in actual motor responses or merely in tendencies to movement. The degrees of response vary greatly. A tendency toward movement may be described as a motor set or pattern which must precede any overt action. It must be emphasized that it is not necessary that we should first have the idea of the formation of such a figure, and that we then imitate in ourselves such a process as Lipps and others have contended. An idea of mechanical construction as "mere idea" is meaningless. Even if the idea of construction were a necessary link, it would itself have to be expressed in motor set and accompanying sensations, for that is the only way in which it could be understood.

Further, these sensations of movement or tendencies to movement are projected into the lines and shapes. They are not felt as movements of our body, but fuse with the object as visual, auditory, or other form of perception, giving character and meaning to the object as will be shown by examples. They are also the cause of the accompanying enjoyment or affective tone. The objects cannot be pleasing unless they give rise to unified empathic responses because the nervous set requires such unification, and that is the ultimate reason why unity in the object is essential to beauty. The degree of unity required in the object for the greatest pleasure, however, depends upon the total situation,[1] and the exact nature of the empathic response, which the particular object induces, and of the consequent perception depends upon the experience and total state of the observer's organism at the time.

It is evident that mere adaptation to the situation, quickly and readily attained through previous familiarity with the perceived objects, would soon lose its interest for us. We do not find pleasure in the accustomed. There must be something present in our relation to the environment that requires a new effort on our part.[2] It may be stated then that a *new* and *successful* adaptation is a necessary and fundamental factor of the pleasure in æsthetic creations.

The following is a description of the motor set from the physiological side. Dr. E. J. Kempf writes: "This is virtually saying that we think with our muscles, because the kinesthetic impulses . . . arising from the embedded proprioceptors are much more numerous than all the others. For example, if we allow ourselves to become aware of the visual image of a moving automobile, the awareness of its movement is furnished by ex-

---

[1] This phase of the problem will be considered in more detail in the chapter on " Unity and Imagination."

[2] Professor R. S. Woodworth has stated, in his *Dynamic Psychology*, p. 102, "Action that is too easy because all difficulties have been smoothed away or already subjugated by well-formed habits is automatic rather than interesting, and action that meets with unsurmountable obstacles is distinctly annoying; but action that encounters resistance but overcomes it without resorting to the last ounce of effort is distinctly interesting."

trinsic muscles of the eye-ball as they shift the image by shifting their postural tensions. Overt movements are not necessary unless we desire a very vivid image, then, also, the muscles of the neck may contribute by moving the head. If the image of the moving automobile is one of ourselves pushing it, then the muscles of the body come into play to furnish the images . . . and, if it is to include pushing it through a cold, wet, muddy road, the sensations of coldness and wetness arise from the tactile receptors of the skin of our legs. If the description of the experience includes the reproduction of an accident (say slipping), we feel the image of the movement of the slipping in our legs first, the remainder of the body then adjusting and coördinating to the change of posture." [1] The possibility of the shifting of tensions in muscles without overt movement gives a physiological explanation of what is meant by the change in tendency to movement and in motor set. This is particularly important, because it has been argued against empathy that the time of perception is often too short for actual movements, and yet within that time effects are observed which are claimed to be caused by an empathic attitude. If it were necessary to make actual movements in order to empathize, then there would be a justified skepticism in regard to the validity of the theory, for it is more than prob-

[1] "The Autonomic Functions and the Personality," *Nervous and Mental Disease Monograph*, series 28, 1918, p. 23.

able that in the majority of instances of empathy no overt action can be detected. Dr. Kempf has written further on this point: "Apparently we may have such changes in the postural tonus as reciprocally increasing or decreasing tonus between the flexors and extensors, pronators and supinators, abductors and adductors of a limb or several limbs without overt movement of the limb; as when one makes his arm give him the sensations of wielding a tennis racket without going through visible movements; and as the sensations of such movements are made more vivid the overt movements begin to appear." [1]

Another argument that has been made against empathy is that it is often impossible to move in the way that perceived shapes suggest. Particular reference has been made to eye movements, the importance of which has perhaps been somewhat overemphasized. It was supposed at one time that we experienced the quality of lines and judged the degree of their gracefulness, etc., by following them with the eyes. Professor G. M. Stratton performed the experiment of photographing the movements of the eyes while they were following a curved line. It was found that they could not trace the curved line but moved in jerks, forming a line with sharp angles which no one could fail to consider disagreeable.[2] That the eye does ordi-

---

[1] *Op. cit.*, p. 21.
[2] "Eye-Movements and the Æsthetics of Visual Form," *Philosophische Studien*, vol. 20, pp. 336–359.

narily move in jerks has been substantiated by other investigators. That it cannot possibly move in smooth curves does not seem to have as yet been conclusively proven. However, these results do not minimize the importance of empathy. It is not necessary to empathize with the eyes any more than it is necessary to imagine ourselves walking in a spiral in order to appreciate the curves. A tendency to move any part of the body that is capable of moving in the way suggested is sufficient. Just what part of the body is used depends upon conditions. We may have the impulse to trace the line with the foot or with the whole leg, or with the hand. We may incline the body or merely the head to one side, we may beat the rhythm with the foot, the head, the hand, or the finger, or the response may come through the change in breathing. The perception of weight may be due to strain in all the muscles of the body which would ordinarily be used to lift an object like the one perceived, or the strain may be in only one small muscle group, such as that which moves the finger.

It must be repeated, in order that there shall be no misunderstanding, that in all such instances, the impulses may be so far in the initial stage that there is no movement produced and frequently not even a consciousness of strain or of other similar sensations. The nervous set is capable of influencing perception, even though it remains completely unconscious and is discoverable only when the conditions are suddenly altered, as in the example on page 111. Professor Titchener, who believes that the effect of empathy can be the result of unconscious processes has written in another connection: "We have learned, again, that physiological conditions may produce their effect not within but upon consciousness; that nervous sets and tendencies may direct the course of conscious processes without setting up new and special processes of their own. . . ." [1]

§ 4. DESCRIPTION OF EMPATHY BY ART CRITICS

In the writings of artists one finds many references to empathic responses. In fact, their descriptions are very frequently in terms of movement and sensations of strain and touch, although as a rule they have not analyzed their attitude so completely in psychological terms, as has Mr. Bernard Berenson who has stated: "To realize the play of muscles everywhere, to get the full sense of the various pressures and resistances, to receive the direct inspiration of the energy expended, we must have the nude; for here alone can we watch those tautnesses of muscle and those stretchings and relaxings and ripplings of skin which, translated into similar strains in our own person, make us fully realize movement." [2] Mr. Berenson distinguishes between actual sensations of strain and pressure in the muscles such as he would have

---

[1] *Experimental Psychology of the Thought Processes*, p. 32.
[2] *The Florentine Painters of the Renaissance*, pp. 86–87. See also pp. 50–56.

in viewing two men wrestling, and which would be too fatiguing for artistic enjoyment, and the imagination of movement suggested by the lines of a statue. Such images of movement he terms "movement values," just as he uses the term "tactile values" for the sensations he gets in fingers and palm, when in his imagination he runs his hands over the lines and surfaces, and thus perceives their true form. What Mr. Berenson prefers to call "imagination of movement," is probably identical with the incipient tendencies to movement and motor set as described above. Mr. Berenson has relied greatly upon these values, and it is undoubtedly in part due to the prominence he has given them in his own consciousness that he is the most unerring of modern art critics, for it is through the muscle sensations that we can, with practice, make the finest discrimination of line and shape, although the clue to such discriminations will appear to come directly through the eye.

The Japanese have always been particularly successful in imparting meaning through very subtle differences in line and shape as well as tone. They have been especially successful in imparting life and motion to their lines whether they represent growing things as trees and grass, or moving objects such as waves of the sea or graceful floating draperies or other inanimate objects of which motion is an essential characteristic. In view of this talent, it seems worth while to quote at length from a description of the instructions which are imparted to the Japanese students in order to make them proficient in this art: "A distinguishing feature in Japanese painting is the strength of the brush stroke, technically called *fude no chikara* or *fude no ikioi*. When representing an object suggesting strength, such, for instance, as a rocky cliff, the beak or talons of a bird, the tiger's claws, or the limbs and branches of a tree, the moment the brush is applied the sentiment of strength must be invoked and felt throughout the artist's system and imparted through his arm and hand to the brush, and so transmitted into the object painted; and this nervous current must be continuous and of equal intensity while the work proceeds. If the tree's limbs or branches in a painting by a Kano artist be examined, it will astonish any one to perceive the vital force that has been infused into them. Even the smallest twigs appear filled with the power of growth—all the result of *fude no chikara*. Indeed, when this principle is understood, and in the light of it the trees of many of the Italian and French artists are critically viewed, they appear flabby, lifeless, and as though they had been done with a feather. They lack that vigor which is attained only by *fude no chikara*, or brush strength.

"In writing Chinese characters in the REI SHO manner this same principle is carefully inculcated. The characters must be executed with the feeling of their being carved on stone or engraved on steel—such must be the force transmitted through the arm and hand to the brush. Thus executed the writings seem imbued with living strength.

"It is related of Chinanpin, the great Chinese painter, that an art student having applied to him for instruction, he painted an orchid plant and told the student to copy it. The student did so to his own satisfaction, but the master told him he was far away from what was most essential. Again and again, during several months, the orchid was reproduced, each time an improvement on the previous effort, but never meeting with the master's approval. Finally Chinanpin explained as follows: The long, blade-like leaves of the orchid may droop toward the earth, but they all long to point to the sky, and this tendency is called cloud-longing (BO UN) in art. When, therefore, the tip of the long slender leaf is reached by the brush the artist must feel that the same is longing to point to the clouds. Thus painted, the true spirit and living force (*kokoromochi*) of the plant are preserved." [1]

Comments are not necessary. It is very evident the student is encouraged to cultivate to a high degree the empathic attitude. The following description from the pen of Kenyon Cox, although not referring directly to empathy, shows without doubt that the artist has cultivated a very strong motor adjustment: "Straight lines will always express rigidity and stiffness while curves will express some sort of growth or motion; . . . The

[1] *On the Laws of Japanese Painting*, by Henry P. Bowie, pp. 35–36.

horizontal line is always suggestive of repose; it is the line of resting water, of the earth of alluvial plains, of everything that has reached a state of equilibrium. The vertical line is a line of stability, of direct opposition to the force of gravity, of strength and vigor. . . . In the double or S-shaped curve, unless it is very restrained in its degree of curvature, there is nearly always a sense of voluptuousness and floridity which may sink to feebleness and aimlessness, like a limp string. It is the characteristic line of the baroque and the rococo. . . . All these characters of lines may be the result of association, or they may have some deeper reason, but they are there, in the lines themselves, without regard to what the lines may be used to represent, and are among the most valuable means of artistic expression." [1]

It is interesting to note the feelings such as "feebleness and aimlessness" which the quality of the movements suggest.[2] It is these induced feelings which underlie much of what is meant by the spirit of various forms of architecture. The

---

[1] *Concerning Painting*, pp. 45–46.

[2] Dr. Helge Lundholm is at present engaged at the Harvard Psychological Laboratory in an investigation of the empathic response to various lines. He has found that certain curves seem to represent more rapid movement than others. Different moods can also be induced in the observer, according to the degree of curvature and angularity of the lines. Furthermore there is a general agreement in the response of those taking part in the experiment when they are asked to draw a line which is sad, joyous, angry, lazy, etc. In Dr. Lundholm's book *Om Objektiva Faktorer I Konsten*, pp. 46–93, there is an introspective account of the effect of lines. This book has not, as yet, been translated.

perpendicular lines of the Gothic as given in the tall, thin columns and the upward curve of the arches, arouse in many persons the mood described as "spiritual," a mood which is felt as an intrinsic characteristic of such construction. The eye follows the unbroken line skyward and one feels the uplift of the walls and columns. This is also seen in Gothic figures where the height is often somewhat accentuated in relation to the width and the folds of the dress fall in unbroken perpendicular lines. There is even an avoidance of any hint toward the horizontal in the arms and legs, which are modelled in straight lines without bend at elbow and knee. If we turn quickly from a photograph of a Gothic interior to one of the Renaissance, there is an empathic shock. In the latter, the horizontal is almost purposely emphasized, and one feels the breadth and the weight. The same is to some extent true also in the Renaissance sculpture, and in the figures portrayed in the paintings of the period. We feel ourselves drawn more toward the earth than in the perception of the Gothic. The Renaissance palaces of Florence, as for instance that of Palazzo Riccardi, give us most decidedly this feeling and when we analyze the construction, we observe that the sweep upward is broken by the horizontal molding on the façade which marks the various floors. It may be that the desire honestly to express the interior arrangement of the various floors is one reason for the addition of the molding, but the effect produced, that of breadth and repose rather than height and aspiration, is too closely related to the spirit of the time as shown in all its other forms of art not to be the chief motive for this construction.

It must be added that some persons do not get the upward thrust of the Gothic as just described, especially those who are accustomed to think of the force of gravity whenever they view architectural construction. For them the thrust is always downward, and although they get the effect of the perpendicular, they do not get that feeling of relative lightness which is caused by the upward movement counteracting gravity. For them the Gothic must have a very different meaning, and this is one more instance of the dependence of the appeal upon the particular adjustment of the individual. Indeed, if it were not for these differences the change in art forms would have been very much slower.[1]

[1] Alexander Bain in *The Sense and the Intellect* has referred in several places to the effect of ideas of muscular exertion upon our appreciation of objects of beauty. On page 361 he writes: "Having experience of the weight of a piece of stone of a certain appearance, we associate the appearance with the weight, the one suggesting the other; so with hardness or tenacity. In this way, we have an associated connexion between substances and their uses founded on these properties. We acquire a strong feeling of the difference between timber and stone, and between stone and metal, and demand that each should be differently proportioned in all kinds of erections and mechanical operations. It has been remarked that our sense of Architectural proportions is founded on our experience of stone, and would require to be re-adjusted if iron were as universally employed." There is a similar reference on page 577 and in *The Emotions and the Will*, pages 242–244, there is a description of the rôle that perception of the force of gravity plays in the "beauty of support."

If one turns to an art historian, such as Professor Wölfflin, who studies the development of moods and feelings in art, and who has the insight to portray the personality of the artist as expressed in his art, rather than in his domestic altercations and butcher's bills, one finds in almost every page of his books some intimation of the dynamic force in paintings, architecture and sculpture as realized through empathy. To select a description at random, that of the Sistine Madonna in Dresden, one reads: "No longer seated on the clouds, as in the case of the Madonna di Foligno, but rather standing erect, floating above the clouds as a vision which can be seen for a moment, only . . . thus did Raphael paint the Madonna. . . . The direct emergence out of the picture, the spring at the spectator must always be connected with an unpleasant impression, . . . The *motif* of progression is a wonderfully light swaying walk. The analysis of the unusual relations of balance in her body, the direction of the lines in the widely flowing mantle, and the gown rustling backward are only in part an explanation of the remarkable effect; it is of importance that the saints to the right and left do not kneel on the clouds, but sink into them. . . ." [1] Those who have attended Professor Wölfflin's lectures and have observed the manner in which he uses his hands and arms, and inclines his head from side to side, as he describes the pictures, know that he first feels himself the light and

[1] *Die Klassische Kunst*, pp. 124–5.

floating walk, the tri-dimensionality, the solidity, the tautnesses of muscle, the expression of the hands, and the countless other dynamic features that he has found of importance in the study of the various periods in the history of art.

Students of rhetoric will recall A. S. Hill's remarks upon what Ruskin terms the "pathetic fallacy," which is the means by which "writers of artistic description sometimes undertake to transfer their emotions to inanimate objects." [1] Among the examples which Ruskin gives is one from Alton Locke:

> " They rowed her in across the rolling foam—
> The cruel, crawling foam."

It is quite evident that the poet's impression here described is produced by empathic response. "The foam is not cruel, neither does it crawl," adds Ruskin, who, not realizing that this projection of one's own set in the inanimate object is the usual attitude, to a certain extent condemns as false such forms of expression. He believes that "We shall find the greatest poets do not often admit this kind of falseness . . . that it is only the second order of poets who much delight in it." But as Hill says, "Here as elsewhere, Mr. Ruskin is so eager to express his views strongly, that he says more than he means." [2] Knowing that Ruskin with his highly developed artistic sense

[1] *Principles of Rhetoric*, p. 257.
[2] *Ibid*, p. 261.

must inevitably have felt the dynamic quality of architecture, and that it would appear in his writings, it was only necessary for us to take down one of Ruskin's books to find a passage such as the following: "Many of us are familiar with the ordinary form of the Italian bell tower or campanile. From the eighth century to the thirteenth there was little change in that form; four-square, *rising high*, and without tapering into the air, story above story, they *stood* like giants in the quiet fields. . . . Their ruins still *frown* along the crests of every promontory of the Apennines." [1]

Probably one of the most vivid experiences of empathy that we can have is in perceiving an object that we realize is not well-balanced and may fall at any moment, as for instance, in witnessing one acrobat balancing another at the end of a long pole. As the acrobat in the air sways back and forth on the verge of plunging head first into the orchestra, the audience goes through at low tension all of his contortions.[2]   Whenever the balance is insecure, the empathic response will, as a rule, be of an unpleasant nature, a fact which the artist does not always bear sufficiently in mind. Even Michael Angelo, in his superb de Medici monument, did not make the support for the limbs of the recum-

---

[1] "*The Seven Lamps of Architecture*, section entitled, "Lectures on Architecture and Painting," p. 238.   (Italics not in the original.)

[2] Adam Smith in his chapter on "Sympathy" has described the writhing and twisting of a mob in watching a slack-rope dancer. . He does not, however, develop this idea further in the direction of empathy. (*Moral Sentiments*, sec. 1, chap. 1.)

bent figures on the tomb of Lorenzo de Medici sufficiently evident, so that for some observers the figures seem about to slip off the incline.

In the drama, the empathy is always very strong, and for the correct æsthetic attitude, we should empathize in all the characters as they in turn take up the action. This usually happens when one is entirely absorbed in the play. At times, however, the character is portrayed in a manner foreign to our experience or understanding. In that case it is impossible for us to respond empathically, that is, to live in the character. The effect on the observer is unpleasant. The character is judged to be badly drawn and untrue to life.

The term "sympathy" may be used by some persons uncritically in instances such as that just described. We may say that we are not in sympathy with the play or the actors, but strictly speaking, sympathy should not be confused with empathy. The latter is feeling in the object. One's own personality is merged and fused in that of some external thing. Sympathy is feeling with; instead of being merged in the object, our feelings run, so to speak, parallel with the object. The difference between the one sympathizing and the object of sympathy is always somewhat present in consciousness. The ego is to some extent represented in consciousness in the form of self-satisfaction, so that the sympathetic response can never be an æsthetic one. One's sympathy is usually expressed in terms of subject and object:

"I sympathize sincerely with you," while one's empathy is in terms of the object: "the man walks awkwardly."

§ 5. GRACEFULNESS

A very evident example of empathy is that of the perception of gracefulness in objects. A graceful motion, as Spencer correctly explained, is a "motion that is effected with economy of force; grace, as applied to animal form, describes forms capable of this economy; grace, as applied to postures, describes postures which may be maintained with this economy; and grace, as applied to inanimate objects, describes such as exhibit certain analogies to these attitudes and forms." [1] Spencer did not specifically mention empathy in this connection but he clearly indicated such a process when he wrote: "How trees and inanimate objects should come to have this epithet applied to them, seems less obvious. But remembrance of the fact that we commonly, and perhaps unavoidably, regard all objects under a certain anthropomorphic aspect, will help us to understand it. The stiff branch of an oak tree standing out at right angles to the trunk, gives us a vague notion of great force expended to keep it in that position; and we call it ungraceful, under the same feeling that we call the holding out an arm at right angles to the body

[1] "Gracefulness," first published in the *Leader* for December 25, 1852. *Essays; Scientific, Political, and Speculative*, Williams and Norgate, 1901, p. 381.

ungraceful. Conversely, the lax drooping boughs
of a weeping-willow are vaguely associated with
limbs in attitudes requiring little effort to maintain
them; and the term graceful, by which we describe
these, we apply by metaphor to the boughs of
the willow." [1] That it is easier to move in sweep-
ing curves than in abrupt turns, is very evident,
so that when we speak of a graceful curve, our
reference is ultimately to our own movement as
suggested by the line. The awkward skater, who
half falls and half slips, arouses such movement
in the observer and the perception is a painful
one. The riding instructor admonishes his pupil
against flapping his arms up and down in riding.
The correct attitude, as dictated by the laws of
grace, is to avoid all unnecessary movement, to
sit quietly in the saddle so that one's movements
coincide with those of the horse. This requires
some skill, but when attained it is a joy to the empathic observer.

The fewer movements a bird makes in flying,
the greater the pleasure to the eye, and when it
soars without any visible movement of its wings
it gives one a keen delight. The sight of an air-
plane in flight gives one a similar pleasure. The observer cannot see the movement of the motor;
the machine glides through the air without apparent effort, just as one would most desire to move,
and the effect is of that highly pleasurable quality
which is experienced in dream flights. The fancy

[1] *Op. cit.*, pp. 385–386.

skater aims at the same economy of effort and the nearer he comes to it, the more highly his skill is praised. Mr. George H. Browne, an expert skater and judge of contests, offers testimony in regard to empathy: "My own experience in judging skating competitions is in complete accord with this [concept of empathy]; my empathetic participation in the action frequently is so intense that awkward movements or unexpected inefficiencies in the contestants almost give me physical pain; if seated, I often find myself on the very edge of my chair; if on my skates, I can hardly keep still; and sometimes I have to exert strong will, not always successfully, to keep from making some audible or active demonstration. I doubt if the winners . . . got much more æsthetic pleasure out of their actual performance, . . . than I did in following 'empathetically' their brilliant program." [1] Mr. Browne has made a study of the graceful movements of swimmers and skaters, and has interviewed several of them. The most famous woman swimmer said of her art: "'I depend on no one part of the body, but in all parts relatively to the whole.[2] *The beauty of movement depends on the success of its muscular economy.* In diving, the grace of movement lasts from beginning to end, when, *e. g.*, the line formed by the body completes itself in the air and the body enters the

[1] *The Æsthetics of Motion*, pp. 31–32.
[2] This is an important point relative to the enjoyment of unity.

water without a splash—then it is a finished performance.'" [1]

The movements of the snake are for many very fascinating. Here one empathizes in the movement of an animal which arouses no movements in one's own legs, yet conveys the idea of motion. When a man or animal is of such weight that one knows from experience that its locomotion will be difficult, then the impression conveyed is one of awkwardness. The empathic response is painful even before the creature moves. The mere sight of the rhinoceros, to use the amusing example of Spencer, is unpleasant as compared with that of a race-horse.

The acrobat attempts to eliminate all signs of effort from his facial expression. As a rule he smiles during his performance thus increasing the impression of ease. If he shows signs of heavy breathing or wrinkles his brow in effort, etc., the act does not meet with the approval of the audience. In piano recitals the experienced musician well knows that he should give as little outward expression as possible of the effort with which he must at times strike the keys to produce his loud effects. Therefore, musicians with little muscular strength should not attempt compositions requiring the use of an effort that is beyond their capacity. Unless they are concealed from the audience, they produce the same painful impression

---

[1] *Op. cit.*, p. 35.

as does a golfer who hits beyond his strength at the ball.

The psychological explanation of the perception of grace in inanimate objects differs only slightly from that of the graceful impression made by moving objects. From what has already been stated regarding empathy the manner in which the lines of the object suggest movement to the observer will be understood. Art depends upon such psychological processes to transmit the pleasure of graceful lines and forms.

This chapter has been concerned chiefly in explaining empathy by examples from the visual arts, but it was not the intention to convey the impression that empathy is limited to any special field of art. Auditory as well as visual rhythm is transmitted to the observer by that process. Indeed, empathy is an essential part of musical enjoyment. Perhaps its importance may seem least evident in literature, but even here much of the effect is produced by the dynamic appeal both in the form and content of literary compositions, whether it is prose or poetry.

Fig. 4.—Equestrian statue of General
Colleoni, Venice.

Fig. 5.—Metope from Selinus, Museum,
Palermo.

FIG. 6.—Maiden, Acropolis Museum, Athens.

FIG. 8.—Thorn Extractor, Palazzo dei Conservatori, Rome.

FIG. 7.—Water Carriers, Parthenon Frieze, Acropolis Museum, Athens.

Fig. 9.—David, by Dona-
tello, Bargello, Florence.

Fig. 10.—Moses, by Michael Angelo, San
Pietro in Vincoli, Rome.

Fig. 11.—Aurora, by Guido Reni, Palazzo Rospigliosi, Rome.

Fig. 12.—Pietà, by Perugino, Academy, Florence.

Fig. 13.—Entombment, by Raphael, Villa Borghese, Rome.

Fig. 14.—Madonna and Child, Florentine School, XV Century, Corsini Gallery, Florence.

Fig. 15.—Madonna, Child and Angels, by a pupil of Botticelli, Kaiser Friedrich Museum, Berlin.

Fig. 16.—Holy Family, by a pupil of Botticelli, Pitti Gallery, Florence.

Fig. 17.—Madonna and Child, by Raphael, Kaiser Friedrich Museum, Berlin.

Fig. 18.—Granduca Madonna, by Raphael, Pitti Gallery, Florence.

Fig. 19.—Holy Family, Venetian School, XVI Century, Palazzo dei Conservatori, Rome.

Fig. 20.—Madonna of the Harpies, by Andrea del Sarto, Uffizi, Florence.

Fig. 22.—Spring, by Botticelli, Academy, Florence.

Fig. 23.—Tobias and the Angels, by Botticini, Academy, Florence.

Fig. 21.—St. Lawrence Receiving the Treasures of the Church, by Fra Angelico, Chapel of Nicholas V, Vatican, Rome.

Fig. 24.—David, by Antonio Pollaiuolo, Kaiser Friedrich Museum, Berlin.

Fig. 25.—Isaiah, by Michael Angelo, ceiling of Sistine Chapel, Vatican, Rome.

Fig. 26.—Cumæan Sibyl, by Michael Angelo, ceiling of Sistine Chapel, Vatican, Rome.

FIG. 27.—Portrait of a Young Woman, by a pupil of Botticelli, Kaiser Friedrich Museum, Berlin.

FIG. 28.—Portrait of a Young Woman, by an artist called Amico di Sandro, Pitti Gallery, Florence.

FIG. 29.—Vision of St. Ursula, by Carpaccio, Academy, Venice.

Fig. 30.—St. Sebastian, by Botticelli, Kaiser Friedrich Museum, Berlin.

Fig. 31.—St. Sebastian, by Guido Reni, Palazzo dei Conservatori, Rome.

Fig. 32.—St. Sebastian, ascribed to Pollaiuolo, Pitti Gallery, Florence.

Fig. 33.—Two portraits in Flemish Costume after the manner of Van der Goes, Uffizi, Florence.

Fig. 35.—Coronation, by a follower of Giotto, Sta. Croce, Florence.

Fig. 36.—Coronation, by Botticelli, Academy, Rome.

Fig. 37.—Coronation, by Raphael, Vatican Gallery, Rome.

Fig. 38.—Madonna of Foligno, by Raphael, Vatican Gallery, Rome.

Fig. 39.—Disputa, by Raphael, Vatican, Rome.

Fig. 40.—St. Petronilla, by Guercino,
Palazzo dei Conservatori, Rome.

Fig. 41.—Madonna and Saints, by Ghirlandaio, Uffizi
Gallery, Florence.

Fig. 42.—Madonna and Saints, by Ghirlandaio, Academy,
Florence.

Fig. 43.—Madonna and Saints, by a pupil of Botticelli, Uffizi, Florence.

Fig. 44.—Madonna and Saints, by a pupil of Botticelli, Academy, Florence.

FIG. 45.—Madonna and Saints, by Botticelli,
Kaiser Friedrich Museum, Berlin.

FIG. 46.—Madonna and Saints,
by Filippino Lippi, Uffizi, Florence.

FIG. 47.—Madonna of the Baldacchino,
Pitti Gallery, Florence.

Fig. 48.—Fisherman and the Doge, by
Paris Bordone, Academy, Venice.

Fig. 50.—Visitation, by Albertinelli, Uffizi, Florence.

Fig. 49.—Annunciation, by Andrea del
Sarto, Pitti Gallery, Florence.

Fig. 51.—Communion of St.
Jerome, by Domenichino, Vatican, Rome.

FIG. 52.—Last Judgment, by Fra Angelico,
Academy, Florence.

FIG. 53.—Lunette, by Luca della Robbia, Bargello, Florence.

FIG. 54.—Madonna of the Sack, by Andrea del Sarto, Annunciata, Florence.

FIG. 55.—Deposition, by Fra Bartolommeo, Pitti Gallery, Florence.

Fig. 56.—St. Ann, Virgin and Child, by
Leonardo da Vinci, Louvre, Paris.

Fig. 57.—Creation of Man, by Michael Angelo, ceiling of Sistine
Chapel, Vatican, Rome.

Fig. 58.—Marriage of St. Catherine, by Bernardino
Luini, Museum Poldi-Pezzoli, Milan.

Fig. 59.—Virgin and Child, by Filippo Lippi,
Pitti Gallery, Florence.

FIG. 60.—Birth of the Virgin, by Ghirlandaio, Sta. Maria Novella, Florence.

FIG. 61.—Birth of St. John, by Ghirlandaio, Sta. Maria Novella, Florence.

Fig. 62.—Adoration of the Magi, by
Filippino Lippi, Uffizi, Florence.

Fig. 64.—Adoration of the Shepherds, by
Ghirlandaio, Academy, Florence.

Fig. 63.—Adoration of the Magi, by Fabriano,
Academy, Florence.

Fig. 65.—Miracle of the Holy Cross, by Gentile Bellini, Academy, Venice.

Fig. 66.—Expulsion of Heliodorus from the Temple, by Raphael, Vatican, Rome.

Fig. 67.—St. Jerome Leading the Lion into the Monastery, by Carpaccio, San Giorgio degli Schiavoni, Venice.

Fig. 68.—Madonna Addolorata and Christ with the Cross, by
Bernardino Luini, Museum Poldi-Pezzoli, Milan.

Fig. 69.—Infanta Margareta, by Velasquez,
Prado, Madrid.

CHAPTER VI

ILLUSTRATIONS OF EMPATHY FROM THE FINE ARTS

§ 1. Force and Movement

In order to explain more fully how our empathic reaction is responsible for what is termed style, mode, and feeling in art, and how a knowledge and analysis of this response increases the appreciation, let us examine the empathic suggestions in the lines of some of the better known sculptors and painters.

In the first place, it should be noted that the strength of the empathic response is not determined by the amount of movement represented in the statue or picture. There could scarcely be a stronger empathic reaction than that induced by Verrocchio's statute of General Colleoni in Venice (Fig. 4), which represents the warrior seated on his charger. The horse is not represented as prancing or in rapid motion. The only action conveyed is that of a very slow, forward movement, suggested by the position of the left hind leg and the raising of the left fore leg. It is not so much motion as force that the artist wishes to portray, and that one feels in every line —in the muscles of the horse, especially in the raised leg and the neck, in the tense position of the rider, in his square jaw and the muscles of his face, in the grip of his toes in the stirrup, in the bend of the elbow which points aggressively toward the observer. Even the angular turn of the horse's tail, gives one the sense of power. Nothing can stop either horse or master, and so tense does one become as one stands before it that the enjoyment is almost painful. Not to have such an experience is not to know the Colleoni. How great our reaction is can be most readily observed if we will turn from a photograph of this masterpiece to some of the modern statues of military heroes in our public squares. Our own muscles will relax in response and the figure instead of appearing to be of flesh and bone will seem of hollow lifeless bronze. There is little doubt that the physical strength of the artist is a condition of the amount of empathy suggested, for he must himself feel in his own body the pose of his group. To a weak individual, too violent empathy is painful and is avoided. Statues by women sculptors most frequently show this lack of force. One feels the listless droop of the arm, the lack of weight of the body, and the relatively slight expression in the posture.

This communication of force and motion is not a late development. The early Greeks expressed it very clearly, though sometimes awkwardly, as for instance, in the representation of the battle between Hercules and the Amazon in the Metope from Selinus in the Museum of Palermo (Fig. 5). Not only is there action in the posture of attack,

but we do not obtain the complete effect until
we experience the pressure of the foot of Hercules
upon that of the Amazon, and the grip of the toes
as they bend over her foot. The Greeks of the
classical period indicated very clearly the weight
of the limbs and body and the poise of the head.
If the arm is outstretched, we feel that it is held
up with sufficient strength, but overemphasis of
effort is avoided by not representing the muscles
too realistically. Of the factors which contrib-
uted largely to the impression of lack of effort
is the expression of the face, which in their greatest
works suggested supreme calm. Of the countless
examples of this, mention might be made of the
Venus of Melos in Paris, and of Praxiteles' Hermes
at Olympia. Even the early works suggested this
quality, as in the archaic statue of a maiden at the
Acropolis Museum in Athens (Fig. 6), where the
expression is one of serenity, although the folds
of the dress and the braiding of the hair suggest
a certain restlessness not found in later works, or
in one of the earlier pieces such as the figures of
the water carriers in the Parthenon Frieze in the
Acropolis Museum in Athens (Fig. 7), where we can
empathize in the arms holding the vase and feel
that it is firmly supported, and that it has weight,
and yet not be disturbed by the exertion of the
men, since their faces show no sign of their labor,
and therefore suggest no feeling of effort.

It is only because of this technique that the
Greeks were able to use human figures, as for ex-

ample the Caryatides of the Erectheum, to support the roof of a building. There is sufficient evidence in the body of the women to indicate that a weight is being supported, but the faces are without lines of effort so that one can empathize in them without pain. Thus does one feel the idealism of Greek art. If we compare this treatment with modern conceptions such as the giant figures supporting the front of the Hotel de Ville at Tours, we shall notice that the latter are bent over, with muscles contracted in great lumps, an almost agonized expression on their faces. Although the feeling suggested may to a certain extent typify the spirit of the time, yet it is from such experiences that we generally desire to escape when we turn to the beautiful.

When extreme empathy was wanted, the Greeks could obtain it, as may be seen in the marvelous sweep of the Victory of Samothrace in the Louvre, where we feel the flutter of every fold of the drapery and the wild drive forward against the breeze. The Discus Thrower is another example where strong empathy in the suggested movement is irresistible. A very delightful bit of empathy is that suggested by the statue from the School of Myron, of the Thorn Extractor in the Palazzo dei Conservatori in Rome (Fig. 3). Here the attention is concentrated upon the fingers which grasp the thorn.

At the time of the Renaissance the empathic appeal of the sculptor was very great. For a strong contrast in the motives of works of art, and from this to the difference in the temperaments of artists, as discernible by our active perception, we may compare a statue by Donatello, such as his David in the Bargello in Florence (Fig. 9), with one by Michael Angelo, for instance the statue of Moses in San Pietro in Vincoli in Rome (Fig. 10). Both of them produce an unavoidable empathy in every line. In the Donatello one feels the tilt of the body, the graceful bend of the right arm, the delicate lines of the left arm, the soft folds of the mantle, the dreamy idealism of the face; the slender figure stands firmly poised, assurance and confidence in every curve, yet with all the lightness that expresses the joy of youth and the happiness of being alive. In the Moses the note is one of weight, power, and severity. The muscles of our arms contract, and our feet cling more firmly to the ground, as we view the statue. The figure is huge, powerful, and heavy, and even the mantle over the knee and the massive beard both convey through their suggested weight the idea of the inflexible will of the leader. It is not necessary to know the history of the man. Every line of the figure, as one experiences it, gives an indication of his character and of the idea of which he is a symbol. In both statues the lines alone impart the meaning of the work, which is so different in the two instances, and behind this meaning the temperaments of the two so contrasting artists.

In painting we have also strong sensations of power or of swift irresistible motion, according to the purpose of the artist, and the empathic participation is almost if not quite as complete as it is in statuary. As an illustration of motion, Guido Reni's Aurora in the Palazzo Rospigliosi in Rome (Fig. 11) may be chosen. Not only do we realize the movement of the galloping horses and the rolling clouds, and the wind-tossed robes, but the lines of the composition are for the most part arranged to induce motion in only one direction. Four of the figures, the leading muse, the angel, Apollo, and the muse in the foreground, have outstretched arms which suggest motion toward the right. How very subtle are the directing influences of lines may be seen from the fact that the movement is somewhat retarded by the half-turn toward the left of the bodies of several of the figures. This is undoubtedly done for the sake of unity, but the effect is to cause in us a slight movement in the opposite direction, which somewhat counteracts the main movement.

An interesting contrast effect may be obtained by the examination of Perugino's Pietà in the Academy in Florence (Fig. 12) with Raphael's Entombment in the Villa Borghese in Rome (Fig. 13). The former has used every means to avoid a feeling of weight or unusual use of the muscles. Very little of the body of Christ rests on the lap of the Virgin, and the drapery is so arranged that no strain can be observed. In order to take up the dead weight, figures are placed on either side to hold the head and feet. Even they show no evidence of exertion. This absence is especially noticeable in the figure

which holds the head and shoulders. If we empathize in the supporting arms we feel no effect of
the force of gravity. The hands rest under the
armpits of the Christ, but they do not seem to bear
the weight of the body. The mechanical evidence
of support, nevertheless, is given, as in the case of
the Caryatides, and the eye is satisfied. If this had
not been done, there would be an empathic movement in the opposite direction. The body would
appear to fall and the empathic movement aroused
would be extremely unpleasant. Added to the
lack of muscular strain in the figures is the serenity
of all the faces, so that the atmosphere of the picture is one of calmness and dignity, such as is
found in intense and deeply felt sorrow. Raphael,
on the other hand, represents the body of Christ
being carried by two stalwart men who pull in
opposite directions upon the winding sheet, which
holds the body. Feet are braced firmly, backs are
bent, and the neck muscles stand out in welts. In
harmony with this expression of effort are the signs
of grief on the faces of those about the central
group. The effect on the beholder through participation in this display of active force and emotional
vehemence is very violent. To turn from Perugino to Raphael is like going from the dignified serv-
ice of the church out into the turmoil of an hyster-
ical mob.

§ 2. Weight

A study of the manner in which the different artists have represented the Madonnas holding the Christ-child offers excellent evidence of the various intensities of empathy and their effect upon the spirit of the picture. In the Madonna and Child, of the Florentine School, XV Century (Fig. 14) in the Corsini Gallery in Florence the Child stands on the knee of the Virgin, but there is no impress such as the weight would naturally produce. Given no such clue to weight, we do not react to the force of gravity and accept the fact without uneasiness that the hands of the Madonna, delicately touching the Child as they would grasp the tender stem of a rose, could not possibly steady the stout little body. The same effect is produced in the Madonna, Child and Angels, by a pupil of Botticelli, in the Kaiser Friedrich Museum in Berlin (Fig. 15). Here the Child, again a well-nourished little figure, stands on the arm of the throne, but since the little leg muscles do not indicate action, and since the mantle on which it stands has no impress of weight, we have the pleasant feeling of the Child standing without the necessity of support by the Virgin. Its little outstretched hand rests on the neck-scarf of its Mother, but no downward pull is indicated so that we do not suffer even the slightest distress which a tug at the delicate neck would cause. Unnatural it all is, but done with the evident purpose, which has actually been achieved, of presenting bodies of flesh and blood without the idea of weight. Even more round and heavy is the Child in the Holy Family, by a pupil of Botticelli in the Pitti Gallery in Florence (Fig. 16), but the artist has made even clearer to the observer that the plump little feet make no impress upon the knee of the Virgin. There is no doubt, on the other hand, that the infants in Raphael's pictures have weight. In the picture of the Madonna and Child in the Kaiser Friedrich Museum in Berlin (Fig. 17), there is an impress in the Child's body where it rests on the Virgin's lap. Our hand curves with the Virgin's as it clasps the Child's back; or where in the Granduca Madonna in the Pitti Gallery in Florence (Fig. 18), it forms a seat for the Infant. Compare the bent fingers of the Madonnas in these latter pictures with those of the Madonnas of Botticelli, which are loosely outstretched.

In the Holy Family of the Venetian School, XVI Century, in the Palazzo dei Conservatori in Rome (Fig. 19), we feel the strength in the hands and arms of Joseph as he holds the Child toward the Virgin while she, no longer slight and ethereal, clasps the massive book with an effort that is somewhat unpleasant in such a scene. Andrea del Sarto, in the Madonna of the Harpies in the Uffizi in Florence (Fig. 20), thinking the one hand of the Virgin insufficient to hold the Child, as Raphael thought, places its foot on a stool which is held by her other hand and supported by her knee. In this picture we feel most strongly the force of the living, active

Child, and the efforts of a woman to hold a very large and restless infant. Small wonder that the tired visitor to the gallery finds more rest in the contemplation of a Perugino or a Botticelli than that of a Madonna and Child of a later period.

The manner in which the figures of the picture stand upon the ground has a very strong influence, if not the strongest influence, upon the empathic response, because through the expression of the limbs and especially of the feet, the observer obtains his idea of the force of gravity involved. In the pictures of the earlier periods, as for instance, in Fra Angelico's fresco representing St. Lawrence receiving the Treasures of the Church which is in the Chapel of Nicholas V in the Vatican (Fig. 23), the figures are often robed to cover the feet, and as there is scarcely any outline of the body we are given very little clue as to weight. In such pictures when the legs are exposed, the foot lies flat on the ground with no evidence of pressure, and the muscles of the legs are not indicated. Botticelli and Botticini also purposely avoided a feeling of weight, and examination of the former's Spring (Fig. 21) or the latter's Tobias and the Angels in the Academy in Florence (Fig. 22), will reveal that the figures stand on their toes with as little effort as on their feet. This is especially evident in the Spring. No matter how they stand, no difference is made in the drawing of the legs. The skin is smooth and unbroken by the outlines of contracting muscles. In several of the figures, although they are standing on their toes, the latter are not even bent by the weight, the foot being a straight line from toe to heel. Even the fish that Tobias carries seems to be made of *papier mâché*, if we judge from the manner in which it is held. To add to the effect, the arms and other lines point upward, thus directing the empathy contrary to gravity.

Botticelli and Botticini do achieve the results they desire, for when we empathize in their figures, we float rather than walk. This absence of the feeling of weight, although condemned by some as unnatural and overdrawn, is greatly admired by others, especially those of rather weak physique, who welcome such emancipation as a delightful relief from the burden of their bodies as experienced under real conditions. These artists' neglect of gravitation undoubtedly brings them a measure of unpopularity. For contrast, one has but to turn to Antonio Pollaiuolo's picture of David in the Kaiser Friedrich Museum in Berlin (Fig. 24). The legs are apart, braced to support the body, and the feet grip the ground with the toes bent downward and the big toe somewhat separated from the others. In Botticelli's figures, on the other hand, there is little spread to the toes.

For the strongest empathy one always turns to Michael Angelo. Even in his seated figures, as for instance, the Sibyls and Prophets on the ceiling of the Sistine Chapel in the Vatican, the effect of the weight is very strongly shown in the feet. In the crossed feet of the Prophet Isaiah (Fig. 25), the

toes are almost bent double, although the weight
is only from the hip, and in the Cumæan Sibyl
(Fig. 26) the toes are well spread out. The empathic appeal in the superb balance of forces in the
figures is too well known to require description.
Even such subtle differences in manner of drawing
the toes are sufficient to be perceived, and to act
as important cues for our general attitute toward
the picture, as we can readily convince ourselves
by carefully examining these various paintings.
Frequently it only requires such small differences,
whether in fine arts, music, or in other fields, to
change the entire mood of the work of art.

§ 3. Lines Expressive of Moods

Botticelli and his pupils knew well the value of
the empathic effect of lines upon mood. This is
clearly evident from the clever way in which they
arranged the hair in their portraits. In the Portrait
of a Young Woman, by a pupil of Botticelli in the
Kaiser Friedrich Museum in Berlin (Fig. 27) the
hair has the form of restless waves, and a heavy
braid hangs down on one side. The face is full of
animation and the restlessness we feel in the hair is
in harmony with the temperament of the girl. In
the Portrait of a Young Woman by the artist called
Amico di Sandro in the Pitti in Florence (Fig. 28),
the hair is brushed almost straight back from the
face; only one strand escapes. The woman in the
latter picture is represented in a pensive quiet
mood. Even the dress has few curved lines as com-

pared with that in the former picture where the restlessness in the costume is enhanced by cross-stitch
trimming, and four black strings of a necklace cross
one another. In the latter picture, on the other
hand, the trimming is very plain and a single cord
falls in a straight line from the neck.

Perhaps one of the best examples of calmness,
peace, and spiritual mystery as indicated by lines,
is the Vision of St. Ursula by Carpaccio in the
Academy in Venice (Fig. 29). Almost everywhere
in the picture we move in straight lines which meet
at right angles, and thus impede movement; seldom
is there a curved line. Even the arm under the
Saint's head is bent in a right angle at the wrist and
again at the knuckles. The little body is outstretched under the coverlets with a slight indication of the upturned feet. Fancy the change in
tone if the bed were in rococo style; if garlands
decorated the wall; if the little Saint were curled
up in her bed, and the Angel were flying toward her
instead of standing quietly near the wall.

The portrayal of St. Sebastian's martyrdom by
various artists affords a good opportunity for comparison. The general content of the picture, of a
Saint bound to a tree and pierced by arrows, is the
same in all the pictures. The differences in the
suggested empathy, however, make a varied series,
as for example, Botticelli's picture in the Kaiser
Friedrich Museum in Berlin, the picture ascribed
to Pollaiuolo in the Pitti in Florence, and Guido
Reni's in the Palazzo dei Conservatori in Rome. In

the Botticelli (Fig. 30) the hands are comfortably behind the back, one leg is slightly in front of the other in a restful position, the lines of the body are quiet, and the face is devoid of any expression of pain. In Guido Reni's (Fig. 31) the face is calm with a somewhat ecstatic and sentimentally religious expression; there is no writhing of the body, although the hands are bound in an uncomfortable position above the head, and the folds of the loin cloth are vigorously intertwined. In the Pollaiuolo (Fig. 32), however, the cords about the arms eat into the flesh as the muscles expand with pain, and the body leans forward and to the side in agony. Suffering is depicted upon the face. In the first two pictures, the arrows have plunged deep into the body in numerous places, but this is not felt as particularly disagreeable by the observer since the lines of the body induce no painful response. Pollaiuolo, however, having vividly suggested suffering to the observer, does not dare follow this treatment of the arrows. Instead of there being a half dozen in chest, abdomen, and leg, he has painted only two and these have merely pierced the fleshy part of leg and arm.

The two Portraits in Flemish Costume after the manner of Van der Goes in the Uffizi, Florence (Fig. 33) offer a striking contrast in the treatment of weight, especially in respect to the hands. The man holds a small book firmly grasped in the two hands, but as it is very light, full expression is given to the act of holding the weight. The woman,

however, has an extremely heavy book and as it
would be unpleasant for the observer to feel the
effort necessary to hold it, especially as it concerns
a woman, the hands are folded as in prayer, and
the book rests upon them without bearing down
any more than if it were made of air. That is,
there is nothing in the manner in which the arms
and hands are drawn to indicate that any weight
is being held. Naturalness is again sacrificed in
order to spare the feelings of the observer.

As a last example of the differences in empathy,
attention might be called to the treatment of hands
by the artists of various schools and periods. We
feel that some hands are devoid of all energy, that
they rest flabbily on the arms of chairs, tables, or
in the lap, while others grasp an object with
strength and vigor. A comparison of this difference in treatment by Velasquez and by Van Dyke
is alone almost sufficient, without further analysis
of their pictures, to give us an important and fundamental difference in the characteristics of the
two artists.

CHAPTER VII

UNITY AND IMAGINATION

§ 1. ATTENTION A UNIFYING PROCESS

THE preceding chapter attempted to explain in detail the nature of the motor reaction or set of the organism in perception, and particularly in the enjoyment of beauty, and it has been already stated that the law of unity is a fundamental one in æsthetics because it is also a fundamental law of mind. It will now be possible to show why this is true, and why we desire and search for unity in the objects about us, whether they are natural or artificial.

Whenever the organism is surrounded by one or more objects, it tries to adapt itself to them. That is, it attempts to assume some form of motor attitude toward them. This is commonly known as directing our attention to the object, and the organism is then said to perceive it. The organism cannot assume more than one attitude at a time, if there is a conflict; that is, the nervous system involved in the movement cannot be integrated in two different patterns at once. The attention to different musical compositions involves very different coördinations of empathic responses, but since, normally, the very same muscle groups are employed, it is impossible to listen to two pieces of music simultaneously. Although there are times when we seem to attend to two totally different situations at once, as when we listen to two different conversations, it is probable that an alternation of attention is here involved. It is also possible under certain conditions for one group of muscles to assume one attitude, and another set a different one at the same time, as in automatic writing, where the hand writes while the voice carries on an unrelated conversation; but the individual is conscious of only one of these acts at a time.

When we are confronted with a multiplicity of objects we observe in ourselves a high degree of restlessness. There is a searching among the objects for some resemblance, some means by which they can be related one to another. In the contemplation of the stars, we may for the moment be emotionally stirred by their distance and number, and, because of the lack of form and relation, by the infinite possibilities and mystery of the scene, as Dr. Santayana has pointed out.[1] It is not long, however, before we begin to search for relations between the stars and to group them into various forms, so that we may the more clearly perceive and remember certain portions of the firmament. With what pleasure a child sees for the first time the Dipper, and the various other imaginary forms in the heavens. How much more do we think we understand things when the stars appear to group themselves, and are thus perceived as large units.

[1] *The Sense of Beauty,* pp. 100 *et seq.*

Hours are spent in contemplating the shapes in the flames of an open fire, that is in uniting the outlines into definite forms, or in finding figures in the veining of the marble facings of the fireplace. This, of course, involves imagination, for we supply the images from past experience, through the suggestions offered by the lines, the result being that the lines themselves always appear to be in some way objectively grouped. Indeed, whenever there is a multiplicity of objects we must perceive them as grouped into some form, if we are to perceive them at all clearly, and this unity of form corresponds to that unification of the organism which is necessary in its response. We may then speak of form as the objective correlate of the inner unity of the various muscle-groups of the organism, which may be described figuratively as bearing the same relation to the total response as do the spokes to the whole wheel.

§ 2. Limits to Unification

There is, then, for the mind, always a possibility of unity in multiplicity, and the act of discovering the unity is in itself a pleasure. It will be seen later that the amount of the enjoyment varies with the ease of this act of unification. First it is necessary to inquire whether every multiplicity is capable of unification and to what extent. As has been stated, in order to unify objects, the mind seeks to relate certain of its aspects. Objects, however, as mere units can be brought together in relation through our response. As Dr. Santayana states it: "The elements may be all alike and their only diversity be numerical. This unity will then be merely a sense of their uniformity." [1] But there is a limit to the possibility of such unification, for the objects must not be too numerous. Some of the earliest experiments in the psychological laboratory were devised so as to discover how many dots can be clearly perceived if they have no relation to one another other than the fact that they are visual stimuli of the same quality. Each dot was equally distant from its neighbor. It was found that one can perceive five or six such objects if they are exposed to the eye for only a fraction of a second, and that all beyond this number are not observed. The same was found for letters and numbers when arranged in meaningless order. They could be individually recognized up to six as the outside limit, with certain individual variations. That is, a nervous pattern can be formed and sufficiently integrated for five or six isolated units so that a single response can include this number of units simultaneously. When a series of similar dots, equally spaced, is exposed to the observer for a longer period of time, the mind has a tendency to arrange them into groups, but of not over six units each. There will be a certain quality in the awareness of these groups, a quality of form which makes one feel that the individual elements of the group belong together; and generally it will be observed

[1] *Op. cit.*, p. 97.

that the spatial distance between groups seems to be greater than between individual units of the same group, although the objective distance is the same.[1] When thus grouped, many more units can be perceived, for each group is then perceived as a unit of a higher order. But again, these higher units cannot exceed six, and there is a limit to the formation of successively higher and more complicated unifications, which depends to some extent upon the experience and training of the individual. This psychological law, which is termed "the span of perception," is applicable to all qualities of sensation. One can perceive and distinguish separately five or six sounds without counting or grouping them, such as the striking of the clock. Any number over that we break into groups, as for example, seven strokes into groups of four and three. In fact, in audition there is a strong tendency to subdivide even three or four units into groups. It is seldom that we can hear a short series of sounds without breaking it up into long and short groups with varying degrees of accent. The fact that the ear tends to group sounds and cannot hold more than six has been of fundamental importance in the development of music.

More attention should be given the law in fine arts than it has sometimes received. Frequently too many unrelated or loosely related objects are placed in a picture, and they induce either bewil-

[1] Attention was called to this fact when the perception of the figure on page 25 was described.

derment in the observer or an arbitrary rearrangement by him. The same law obtains in touch, and is one of the reasons why the Braille System for the blind is based upon various arrangements of six raised points, which are felt by the fingers. Since not more than six points are used for one letter, each letter can be felt as a unit. This feature makes the system simpler for the user.

It is clear from the above that when there is unity in multiplicity, as in the repetition of the same letter of the alphabet, there will be a breaking up of this larger unit into smaller groups, As Dr. Santayana has stated, a mere perception of uniformity in a number of units such as a file of soldiers or the railings of a fence is deadly monotonous and not to be endured.[1] If they are not somehow broken into groups, the attention will not be held. The other extreme is entire lack of uniformity, as in the succession of totally different objects. Still, as objects they admit of being grouped and a certain degree of unity may thus be obtained. Between the extremes, there are all degrees of similarity as a basis for unification.[2]

It is probable that when only one physical object is given, there is a search for a relation between its various characteristics, or attributes, which relation gives it structural form or form quality, as it is sometimes expressed.

[1] *Op. cit.*, p. 106.
[2] For unity in multiplicity, see Fechner's *Vorschule der Æsthetik*, part I, pp. 53 *et seq.*

We perceive the relation between the various attributes of a single tone, such as its pitch or place in the scale, its intensity or loudness, its volume, that is whether it seems small as do high tones, or large as do low ones, and its timbre, or the number and quality of its overtones. These attributes are, to an extent, independent variables. They are found in different relations to one another, and give the tone its color or character. The same is true of a single color; the relation of its attributes, such as hue, luminosity, etc., gives the color its form quality. In short, although the perception of tones, colors, etc., seems at first thought a very simple process, it is, in reality, the result of the unification of a number of characteristics; and the pleasure we obtain in such perception depends, to some extent, upon this unity.

There is also present the pleasure of associated ideas; for it must be remembered that the perception of a pure sensation independent of the associated factors is impossible for a mind that has had any experience whatever. A pure sensation would be an experience without any meaning. The natural process of the mind is to relate the present with past experience, which is the basis of recognition and is in the nature of unification. Although most frequently this is carried on in unconscious rather than conscious terms, still there is, at times, a conscious relating with the past. "That is a likeness of ——," is the usual remark on seeing a portrait, and this recognition is generally accompanied by a certain degree of pleasure, as Aristotle pointed out in his attempt to find an explanation for the æsthetic pleasure in the ugly.

If it were not the case that there is such activity in the perception of a so-called simple sensation, it would have to be concluded, either that unity is not fundamental to æsthetic pleasure, or that single sensations such as color, cannot give such pleasure; that there is only pleasure when there is combination of one or more sensations, as pairs of colors, or musical tones. Experience teaches, however, that for many individuals there is a decided pleasure in the presentation of single colors and tones. Nor does it seem necessary to restrict the application of the law of unity by stating that unity plays no part in the enjoyment of a single color in instances where such enjoyment is independent of associated factors, for, as has been stated, it may very well be that the pleasure derived from the contemplation of a colored surface of uniform hue resides in the distinct activity of unifying the different characteristics of the color of the surface.

Even when the pleasure is solely in the purity of the color or tone, the sense of unity is invoked, but it is doubtful whether this is often a source of pleasure, since such contemplation very soon becomes monotonous. Fechner recognized this fact, yet he remarked that "In general the eye likes to rest for some time upon a panel of pure color especially

when the nature of its purity comes to consciousness," etc. [1]

§ 3. UNIFICATION AN ECONOMY OF EFFORT

Beside the pleasure in unifying a series into
groups according to the law of perception, there is
another factor that must be considered, namely,
the principle of economy of effort, which underlies the tendency to form as large a group as we are
capable of perceiving as a whole. Indeed, if this
were not true, why should not the organism adjust
itself separately to each one of a series of dots instead of combining them into groups? It has been
shown that not only are such units combined into
groups, but there is always a tendency to combine
groups into higher groups so as to include more
and more elements under a single heading until,
as in the case of a picture, the parts can all be
grasped simultaneously—that is, until there is finally one total adjustment of the organism in the
perception of the picture.

Generally a name or at least some sort of mental
symbol is given both to small units and to those of
a higher order, so that the mind may, in future
reference, adjust itself instantly to the whole situation through the medium of the symbol instead
of having to recall all of the original process of adjustment, in order to have again the finished perception and the accompanying pleasure. In literary productions this mechanism is especially

[1] *Vorschule der Æsthetik*, p. 59.

obvious. Here we find the letters grouped into words, and these into sentences, paragraphs, chapters, etc., until there is the finished unit of the whole book. To this final result one generally attaches some mental symbol of one's own individual choice, if the book has been successful as a work of art, and has as a finished product offered such total unity. This symbol then acts as a cue for the renewal of that final more or less complete adjustment which one has had at the end of the book, and which underlies what we consider the general impression. This adjustment becomes less and less specific in detail with time, but so long as the general form is preserved and no other factor enters in the meantime, the sense of the original æsthetic value, though not, of course, the vividness of the original æsthetic pleasure, remains as strong as at first. It is not only unnecessary to recall the details of the book, but frequently this is no longer possible, and yet we are just as cognizant of the degree of our pleasure as at the time of finishing the reading—sometimes more so. That such a process is economical is obvious. It is the principle that one finds not only in æsthetic reactions but in all intellectual processes; otherwise it would be impossible for the organism to develop beyond a certain stage, for its mass of past experience, which must be used for future progress, would become overwhelming. The æsthetic unity, therefore, becomes the model for our general activity.

From the foregoing it follows that the mind becomes more highly organized and action becomes more completely systematized the more fully our appreciation of beauty is developed. The æsthetic enjoyment, then, instead of being a mere indulgence, is seen to be the most broadly useful and far-reaching of all our activities. As its influence is felt everywhere, it is not difficult to find an example to illustrate the point. When spending our vacation at the seashore, we may live from moment to moment without a thought or care for the next hour like the victims of mere chance. This may be for some of us a very restful and beneficial attitude, but at the end of the summer our impressions are confused and instead of having any definite and pleasurable reaction, which sums up the whole period of self-indulgence, we are left with a haze of mingled joys and annoyances. If, on the other hand, we have planned our days and weeks, at the end there is a pattern and construction, the realization of which is a source of pleasure, and the memory of which is easily retained as a lasting joy. The vacation has thus been a truly beautiful one and the pleasure obtained becomes the incentive for more valuable achievements. A change of occupation is necessary from time to time; of that there is no doubt, and that is why there are vacations, but to suppose that mere disconnected pleasures are beneficial is contrary to the fundamental law of mind. Such pleasures are detrimental, rather, to complete success in life. It will probably be said that artists are as a class most unsystematic in their lives, and that the law of unity in æsthetics has no influence upon their general behavior.   This is true of many, but the greatest among them have given evidence of a high degree of organization in other fields of activity as well. It is also a fact that those who have shown great executive ability in big business undertakings, which require the highest sense of unity, have, contrary to the general notion of the practical man of affairs, a keen appreciation of beauty.   Many examples could be cited of successful bankers and merchants who spend their spare time in the collection of pictures and in literary pursuits, because of their sense of beauty and not merely for the sake of collecting.   They find in these so-called "hobbies" an opportunity to exercise the same functions that they have learned to recognize as fundamental to their success in business.   In the enjoyment of their hobby they are able to experience the unifying activity in its purity, and with their attention more directly upon it.

§ 4.   Unity of Form and Content

Thus far, the description of unity has been concerned almost entirely with the mental aspect. In regard to this topic, however, as with the previous one of empathy, it is also necessary to describe the other side of the æsthetic relation, namely, that arrangement of the object which is conducive to unity.   There are three separate expressions of unity in most art objects: a unity of form, a unity of content, and a unity between form and content. Unless all three are brought to the greatest perfection, there will not be complete æsthetic enjoyment.

In literature as much insistence has been placed upon the unity of the formal elements as upon that of the meaning. Nevertheless, authors frequently are not sufficiently careful about the arrangement of the words into sentences, paragraphs, etc., nor do they think this important, the interest being primarily upon the meaning underlying the visual symbols. The symbols, however, are related to one another, not only through the ideas for which they stand, but also through their size, spatial relation, sound, accent, etc., that is, as mere sensory impressions stripped of any other meaning, and both of these unities must be strictly considered from the standpoint of art.

Although unity of content has been, for the most part, a comparatively easy factor of attainment, and is always in some degree present in literature, æsthetics has been chiefly concerned with the plot, and has given less consideration to the factor of general mood or peculiar atmosphere of the work of art. For example, the reader is early prepared for light or serious fiction, for a biographical or an historical sketch; in the drama the audience is soon put in the frame of mind for a farce, a light or serious comedy, or a tragedy. It is the writer's task to provide the means by which we may become quickly adjusted to the general mood of the work, and unless the same general tone is maintained throughout, there will be a mental jar, and consequent displeasure analogous to the experience we have if, in following with the eyes the Renaissance lines of a building, we come suddenly upon a Gothic treatment.

It is true that the greatest playwright, Shakespeare, has introduced comic situations into his tragedy, but they are entirely separate from the main plot, and contain characters that do not otherwise appear, and that have no important relation to the other personages of the play. To have one of the principal characters appear now as a serious and now as a comic figure, would be fatal, unless the audience has been prepared for the change by the introduction of some plausible reason for it. As Aristotle has written concerning the unity of character: "The fourth point is consistency: for though the subject of the imitation, who suggested the type, be inconsistent, still he must be consistently inconsistent. As for example. . . . Iphigenia at Aulis,—for Iphigenia the suppliant in no way resembles her later self." [1] Professor George P. Baker has recently called attention to the necessity of this form of unity. "Why is it that a play which begins seriously and for most of its course so develops, only to end farcically, or which begins lightly only to become tragic, leaves us dissatisfied? Because the audience finds it difficult to

[1] *Aristotle's Theory of Poetry and Fine Arts*, translated by S. H. Butcher, p. 55.

readjust its mood as swiftly as does the author. *The Climbers* and *The Girl with the Green Eyes* of Clyde Fitch are examples in point. The first begins with such dignity and mysteriousness that its lighter moods, after Act I, seem almost trivial. In the second play, the very tragic scene of the attempted suicide, after the light comedy touch of the preceding parts, is distinctly jarring." [1]

In the early period of painting, artists sometimes attempted to portray more than one idea. Several events in the life of the Holy Family, for example, are depicted on one canvas, but this is very rarely done in the later periods of art development. Here we find one central idea and even though there may be many figures engaged in various forms of activity, as in pictures by Tenier, where, for example, one finds a group dancing in the foreground and drinking and horseplay in other parts of the scene, still there is a certain unity in the general idea, although this is often so tenuous that it needs to be reinforced by careful balance and other formal factors. Professor Hildebrand has very well expressed the importance of the spatial factors for unity as compared with the unifying power of the subject-matter of the picture. "Consider an imaginary landscape. Here the natural organic coherence is very loose as compared with that of a human body. The trees may stand here or there; the stream may follow this or that

[1] *Dramatic Technique*, p. 111.

course; the hills may stretch thus or so;—it all depends on the artist's choice.   And yet, in a good landscape we are conscious of a certain visual coherence between its parts, making it appear as though it could not be otherwise than it is.   All the details of the picture are mutually conditioned as stimuli so as to produce in our minds a unified whole." [1]

§ 5. Unity Between the Form of Expression and the Meaning

That which is most frequently neglected, is the third factor—the unity between the form of expression and the meaning expressed.   In literature rhythm and sound should, through their emotional value, be related to the ideas for which the sentence stands.   Even the length of paragraphs and the division into chapters or acts bears a decided relation to the contents, and influence the quality of the total æsthetic impression.

The close relation between the form and the content in music, in instances where a content has been considered by the composer, is obvious to persons with even a superficial knowedge of that art.   It is through the emotional effect of the sounds that the ideas are conveyed, such as the voices of the forest, the boom of the sea, or the emotions of love, anger, etc.   There are those who believe that music should be an art of pure form, and this even though they are not members of that radical group

[1] *Problems of Form in Painting and Architecture,* translated by Max Meyer and R. M. Ogden, p. 52.

of persons who desire the principle of "art for art's sake" to be applied to all art. One must balance the gain with the loss. Purely "formal" music may more completely delight, but the joy of the perception of the higher unity of form and expression, and with it that closer touch with life, will be absent. An example of this unity is to be found in song, where the words should be chosen not only for their meaning but for their melodic and rhythmic qualities as well. How important this is, may be seen from the loss in æsthetic effect which often occurs in the translation of songs from one language into another. It is almost impossible, even for the best translator, to obtain the high degree of unity of the original. However, music for the most part is dependent upon its formal elements for its effect. The formal unity is the more important, and has been brought to greater perfection in music than in any of the other forms of beauty. Architecture is very closely related to music in this respect, while painting and sculpture are more akin to literature.

Probably in no art is the unity of content and form closer than in painting. We have evidence from the artist himself that he consciously strives for this result. According to Kenyon Cox, "As soon as any attempt is made to represent the color of objects there is a scheme of coloring which is either harmonious or inharmonious, appropriate or inappropriate. . . . We have seen . . . that the aim of painting is seldom exact imitation and that all the higher qualities of imitative art are dependent upon selection, emphasis, and suppression, that the chosen characters of things may be more instantaneously and more powerfully apprehended than they could be in the presence of the things themselves. These selections, exaggerations, and suppressions are made upon the principle of relational art. The actual shapes and colors of objects are modified to take advantage of the inherent characters of lines and colors. A line is straightened here because straight lines express strength and rigidity, or more curved there because curved lines suggest grace and movement. Colors are intensified to express passion or clarified to give lightness and gayety." [1]

The power of the emotional effects of lines was shown in describing empathy. It was also intimated that this effect should harmonize with the subject-matter of the pictures. The value of this blending is especially clear in the two portraits of young women (Figs. 27 and 28). It was not mere whim or a chance coiffure of the model that caused the artists to adopt the wavy lines for the headdress of the one woman, and the straight lines for that of the other, but the fact that in themselves they expressed the dominant mood which they desired, and which they considered in every detail of the picture.

The greatest of modern portraitists have developed to a high degree this unity of the formal

[1] *Concerning Painting*, pp. 57–58.

effect with the mental characteristics of the subject, and they have thus made their portraits live, as they could have done in no other way. The most careful representation of spatial values and the most faithful portrayal of objects would not have put so much soul into Sargent's portraits as he has obtained by his marvelous selection of proportion and the right balance of color and shade. Other examples of this unity are to be found in the works of the Swedish painter Björk who, by skilful use of line and color, has disclosed with subtlety the inner character of his models. A rather unintelligent, delicate, and kindly young Princess is shown in light blues with a background of fragile Louis XVI furniture. A parvenu and his wife wear rich brown furs, a red Turkish rug lies on the floor and a heavy baroque wardrobe forms an important part of the setting. In another picture a temperamental and highly intellectual young Jewess, in red dress draped in restless folds, is recumbent upon a sofa. Such are some of the more obvious factors which have been employed for their psychological effect. Too much attention cannot be given to these details, where unity is concerned. Even the design and color of the frame should be chosen, not only to blend with the lines and color of the picture, but also with the theme, so far as this is possible.

In statuary and decorative art, the position from which the object is to be viewed must be considered, especially if complete unity is to be obtained. Statuary should be so planned that a unified effect, both as regards lines and subject-matter, can be obtained without the necessity of walking around the group. There should be the possibility of obtaining such a unified perception from at least one point of view. That is, lines and figures essential to the total effect should not, as it were, extend around the corner. [1] If a statue is placed in the center of a square, then each of the four sides should be a complete composition. This is practically impossible, and in consequence Professor Hildebrand, who has insisted that there should be a dominant point of view, condemns the placing of a statue in a position where "all aspects of it are given equal value. . . . As the spectator circles about the statue he has at least four views to take in, and this can be to the advantage of only a very few works and of pleasure, in general, only with figures in the nude." [2]

In large vases there is the same consideration. The Greeks, who understood this principle, arranged the running designs for the most part so that a complete picture could be perceived without moving the head. In smaller vases and other ornaments, this is not of so much importance, since the object can be turned around rapidly in the hand. Even here, however, reservations must be made, as for instance, in regard to the decoration on the covers of books. Although a book is a small object, nevertheless one desires a unified effect as it

---

[1] See Hildebrand, *Problems of Form, etc.,* p. 94, and for examples, Cornelius, *Elementargesetze der Bildenden Kunst,* pp. 26 *et seq.*

[2] *Idem.,* p. 117.

lies closed upon the table. Therefore the design
should be complete on the one side, for otherwise
the book would have to be placed open and face
down, which no book-lover would allow.[1]

In addition to the unity of the spatial factors
and of the ideas which are expressed in sculpture
and the other tri-dimensional arts, there is the
equally important unity of the material in which
the work is executed and the subject represented.
On seeing, say, a Rodin figure in bronze one is apt
to forget that the dark surface and enduring quality of the metal are not there by accident but have
been selected in order best to express the subject
portrayed, until, perchance, one compares it with
the very different but harmonious effect of a slim
Gothic princess in delicate green stone and white
ivory, or is confronted with the less pleasing result
of a similar figure in white marble.

§ 6. Pleasure in the Successful Effort to Unify

That the mind seeks unity is a fact, and that the
object should lend itself readily to unification is
equally true, but the arrangement should not be
such that the unity is thrust upon the mind. Together with pleasure in the unity there is a pleasure
in its attainment. Successful effort is pleasant,
but, just as the joke which is fully explained loses
its effect, so in general the too-obvious is distasteful

---

[1] Professor Cornelius gives illustrations of a book design which observes
this principle and of others which violate it. *Op. cit.*, pp. 41–43.

if not obnoxious. The mind always seeks new worlds to unify. As soon as it has learned readily to harmonize two objects, it desires to include a third. To state the law as a desire for unity in multiplicity is therefore not sufficient. The unity should not be too easily won; and so, since practice brings facility, it often happens that what pleases one to-day will be uninteresting to-morrow. The history of the development of art clearly shows this. If a musical composition is so simple that we can instantly grasp it without effort, it seems to lack that deep pleasure which we desire. In some of our moods it may be pleasant and very harmonious, but beneath it all is the longing for something else. Repose, though it may be sought, is never long enjoyed when once attained. This may seem to some extent at variance with experience, for the mind does avoid difficulties, yet it does this when it is fatigued or when it is being urged to a greater activity than it is capable of attaining. There is no intellect that does not desire to create continually, and the pleasure in the perception of a new or unaccustomed form of unity is comparable to that of original achievement.

A critic, in comparing a certain symphony by Tschaikowsky with one by Beethoven, has said that in the former the construction seems obvious after one has listened to the work of Beethoven in which one continues to find unfamiliar and unexpected intricacies which have to be clarified and understood. The result is that one anticipates a new joy in Beethoven and the renewal of an old pleasure in Tschaikowsky. A sharp contrast is to be had by comparing music of the time of Mozart with modern music of the style of Strauss. To be sure, many listen to Mozart with pleasure, and return to him as to a favorite book, but just as we desire new books and plots with which we are unfamiliar, so we seek new resolutions in music.

This fact of the need of a certain difficulty in unifying, has been of the utmost importance in determining the trend in the development of music.[1] This has perhaps been truer of music than of any other art, although its effect is observed wherever beauty is sought. In everything there is a limit: just as the unity can be too simple to be enduringly satisfactory, so it can be too complex to be understood at certain stages in the development of the individual or the race. It may be not only unsatisfactory, but even decidedly unpleasant. There is here a balance to be considered, as was the case in the amount of the personal appeal in the æsthetic attitude, but in this instance, it is a balance between simplicity and complexity in the act of unifying. No specific rule can be formulated regarding the exact balance to be maintained, for it is of necessity continually changing. It must be determined at any given

---

[1] See the description of experiments made by Professor Henry T. Moore to determine the cause of the changes in the æsthetic perception of musical intervals in "The Genetic Aspect of Consonance and Dissonance," *Psychological Monographs*, No. 73; also his book *The Sense of Pain and Pleasure*, Chapter VIII.

time according to the existing conditions. That it differs in individuals is one of the reasons for the non-conformity of taste. One organism has just sufficient adaptation to music to like ragtime. Another enjoys classical music almost from infancy, and seeks something beyond any existing form. Experience may be depended upon to shift the balance ever toward the complex, though this movement may be almost imperceptible in the æsthetically obtuse. Education in art points out the various factors that should be united and the nature of their harmony, and thus hastens an otherwise spontaneous but slower change.

Most frequently we are not aware that we are unifying, for we do not, as a rule, stop to analyze our perceptions; yet it is the unification that gives us pleasure, and it is this pleasure which has the important position in attention. It is when conditions make this unification difficult that we are most apt to consider what is taking place within us. It has previously been explained that we are usually unaware of our own activity in the empathic response; and in fact a great part of our mental life is unconscious. There are cases of unity which go on entirely unconsciously and which many observers might never understand if they were not explained, such as the blending of small patches of color that are in juxtaposition. A color produced by such blending seems to be more luminous than one produced by the direct mixtures of paint. This method is used by the Pointillists, of whom Monet is the best example, in order to get their sunlight effects. Many persons will have observed the small colored dots on closer inspection of the painting, without having given much thought to the purpose of the method, or the cause of the results obtained; but when one understands that the apparently monochromatic surface is produced through the physiological blending of colors, and that there is thus a unity that one had not before suspected, there. is an added pleasure in the sunlight effects.

In the formal unity there is merely the activity of arranging the various parts according to a plan: and this is all that needs explanation in regard to much of music and to all the purely decorative arts. From what has been said above, it is evident that a simple form of unity is found where there are few elements to be combined, where the form of combination is clearly indicated, and where the unity has been experienced before. The unity becomes more difficult to achieve with an increase in the number of elements, with a decrease in the amount of assistance to unification, and with a decrease in the familiarity of the combination.

§ 7. The Appeal to the Imagination

In the unity of content, the factor of imagination complicates the situation, for here the pleasure is influenced by the amount of appeal to the imaginative processes. In every perception, even the most formal, there is some demand upon the imagination, but in formal art this demand is less than in representative art. In a sense we can call this arousal of the imagination an appeal to our intellectual activity, so that again our pleasure is relative to the degree of activity.

The more fully the object is described, that is the more complete the imitation, the less is the demand upon the activity of the imagination, and

FIG. 34

A drawing in *The Christian Science Monitor* by Frank Bishell

the more sketchy the representation, the more must be supplied by the mind. This is readily seen in that form of sketching in which a few suggestive lines represent a human figure. The small number of lines demands a greater activity on the part of the imagination, and for some persons such a method affords more pleasure than if the entire outline were given. Individuals, however, differ even more in regard to their imaginative response than in their ability to unify discrete elements. Those who belong to the literal type require everything explained most fully. For them each step of an argument must be given, from premise to conclusion. In a description every detail must be included or there is a perplexity which is almost painful, while for others the same argument or description would be too obvious and therefore equally distressing.

There has always been a conflict between realistic and imaginative art, and each has had its followers. Indeed, a person's preference varies with his mood, and his change of mood is frequently conditioned by a surfeit of one or the other form of representation. In the matter of stage-setting realism leaves very little to the imagination. One recalls Mr. Belasco's meticulous attention to details. If a parlor of the "Early Grant" period is to be represented, the family albums, shells, peacocks' tails, daguerreotypes, must all be there; the clock must not only be at the proper hour, but must run according to the lapse of time on the stage; the calendar must be on the wall and turned to the proper date; in short, no chance must be taken that any one in the audience will miss an accustomed object. The pleasure lies in the fact that everything is completely represented, and where that is the purpose the greatest care must be taken to carry out the scheme.

Such details, however, may become wearisome. The mind often rebels at having everything prepared for it, for this is almost like an insult to the intellect, or more specifically, to the imagination. It may then be a relief to return at times to the Elizabethan manner of stage-setting, where one is stimulated to imagine the scenery by mere signs, such as "This is a wall." Suggestion of scenic effect has here reached its minimum, and the richness of the scene depends entirely upon the observer. Modern scenic artists, who have reacted against extreme realism, although for the most part they have not returned to the Elizabethan form, have presented those features only which are essential for the general idea, depending upon the audience to fill in the gaps. Instead of representing a hotel lobby with the accustomed details, there may be merely a back drop representing the windows of a dining room, with drawn shades, and a couple of benches in front of the windows. The lights and sounds of voices convey the idea of many guests in the dining room. The spaces on either side of the drop indicate that there are corridors and from the context of the plot one soon imagines numerous rooms leading off from them. There is no one without some degree of imagination, but some have so little that such a scene will appear barren and stupid. To the highly imaginative, however, it will be richer in effect than the more realistic scene in which the very details impede the imagination of the observer.

It is, however, not true that those who enjoy realism are always without imagination, for some

desire realism because they seek in art a close imitation of nature, thus confusing a truthful representation with a beautiful one. The stage setting
just described will be displeasing to them because
it is not an exact representation of what they have
been accustomed to think of as a hotel lobby, and
not because they cannot imagine such a lobby if
they will. Nevertheless, there will probably be
found a close correspondence between the relatively non-imaginative and those who insist on
realistic art.

§ 8. Degrees of Appeal to the Imagination

A survey of the forms and degrees of activity mentioned above may very well be made by describing
three different styles of pictures. Let us suppose
that the first is a realistic representation of still
life: a simple group of pears, an apple, orange, and
banana. The formal unity will be easily grasped,
but the content is meager and there is for that reason little left for the imagination. The picture is
pleasingly decorative perhaps, but we do not study
it long. It is true that the imagination may wander
into Italy and enjoy that climate, but then we have
left the picture. Music strongly stimulates the
imagination in just this way. In listening to a
symphony, our mind frequently becomes intensely
active, but, alas, how often has the attention wan-
dered from the music to some irrelevant topic.

A second picture is also one of still life, but with
many objects represented, as for example one of

Snyders', where a butcher shop is represented with the various meats in gruesome details. The composition is clever and intricate and there is greater opportunity for unifying both form and content than in the former picture, but there is still little left for the imagination. In fact, there is much included that the imagination of some, if left unguided, would not have cared to supply.

A third picture will be found to have a seemingly very simple arrangement of lines and masses, and the effect will depend entirely upon how successfully these few details are able to suggest the intended scene. If we look closely at the picture by Whistler of the Thames at night, we shall see only blotches of dark gray paint of different intensity, which do not seem to have any definite form. If we retreat about four feet from the canvas, we perceive the most beautiful nocturne. As if by magic we see before us the bridge, the sweep of the river, the reflection of light upon the water, and the small boats with points of light at the portholes. Every object is most easily recognized, and the total effect is one of great beauty, for the mystery of the night is portrayed in a manner which few artists have been able to attain. How much has been left to the imagination is here little realized unless we have closely inspected the canvas, so entirely unconscious are we of our active participation.

Whistler is probably one of the best examples of an artist who obtains a rich content with a mini-

mum of visual cues. To express oneself clearly in a
few words is much more difficult than by the use
of complex sentences, and so it is in fine arts, in fact
in every art. Whistler has been able almost entirely by the subtle gradation of grays to represent
the quality of depth in his pictures to a degree that
even some of the best artists have been able to ac-
complish only by the employment of every known
factor of experience, such as perspective, difference
in size, color, etc. To achieve this there is most
delicate differentiation of brightness values from
point to point in space, such as is also seen in the
paintings of the Japanese, who also are masters of
this seeming simplicity in form. In rendering
shapes, Whistler also gave only the barest indication of what he wanted to be perceived but there is
just sufficient to evoke the perceptions of bridges,
boats, and water most vividly, as soon as one is
sufficiently far away not to recognize the small,
irregular brush strokes of dark paint for what they
actually are. Only a genius after years of study can
obtain such simplicity in the form of expression,
yet so little has this been understood at times, that
Whistler had to sue one of his patrons for the price
of a picture because the patron contended that to
put a few dabs of paint upon the canvas could not
have taken many hours.

No less skilful is the poet in the appeal to the
imagination. Could a hundred lines be more descriptive than these few words:

"Circumstance
Upon the maple leaves
The dew shines red,
But on the lotus blossom
It has the pale transparence of tears." [1]

Frequent mention has been made of cues which the artist employs, and it was stated that these cues—lines, shapes, colors, etc.,—call up a meaning somewhat as the printed word does; but in the search for simplicity of expression it should not be forgotten that such cues must be typical and more or less customary ones as words are, or they will fail to stimulate the imagination in the direction desired by the artist. They cannot be cues which happen to please the caprice of the artist, but rather those which the mind is accustomed to associate with the object intended, through long practice. A child, for example, when it commences to draw, will probably represent a box merely by a rectangle; but it will soon learn to sketch the box according to a plan that is easily recognized by others. For every object, there are developed forms of representation that portray that object in distinctive positions—that is, in positions which differentiate it from other objects, and these forms become the signs or cues for the object. A circle, for instance, is a shape that belongs to hundreds of objects; without shading or detail, it would represent a dollar, the moon, the earth, etc. Out of the countless possibilities, therefore, what chance

[1] From Amy Lowell, *Pictures of the Floating World*, p. 4.

is there that it would suggest an egg to any one, yet it is the outline of an egg as seen with the end toward the observer. An ovoid, on the other hand, is the shape of fewer objects, and is therefore adopted as the normal aspect of the egg, and is used to represent it. This is a very evident example to illustrate that the artist, when he is engaged in simplifying his forms or developing new ones, must always keep in mind the necessity of communicating his meaning to others in an unequivocal manner.

CHAPTER VIII

ILLUSTRATIONS OF UNITY FROM THE FINE ARTS

§ 1. Direction of the Attention Suggested by the Lines

The manner in which the artist arranges his composition in order to produce a unified perception will be described by illustrations from the fine arts. It will also be shown how the empathic responses to the picture are coördinated about the central theme so that after the different parts have come clearly to the attention, the total picture is immediately and clearly perceived.

A very serious problem that the Italian painters had to meet regarding unity was that of joining the terrestrial with the celestial events. Some artists were not at all able to solve it, with the result that one actually had two pictures. In most of the paintings, however, we see some attempt. The crudest method was to have parts of the two worlds interlaced or dovetailed. This was almost always· accompanied by some suggestive lines or cues for directing the gaze. The guiding of the attention is the more subtle form, and is more highly developed in the later paintings. Such a unity has a more spiritual effect than that produced by the overlapping or juxtaposition of lines.

In the picture of the Coronation by a follower
of Giotto in the Church of Sta. Croce, in Florence
(Fig. 35), the artist avoided the problem by representing the heavenly scene only—Christ, the Virgin,
and four Angels. An example of the cruder form of
the unity of the two worlds is found in Botticelli's
Coronation of the Virgin, in the Academy in Florence (Fig. 36). The Angels floating in the heavens,
almost touch the heads of the Saints. The hands
of the Saints at either side of the picture point
to the heavenly scene, and give direction to the
attention, but the figures are not well coördinated and we do not feel strongly impelled by
the gaze of the Saints to look heavenward. Raphael's Coronation in the Vatican Gallery in Rome
(Fig. 37), portrays heaven and earth completely divided by a horizontal strip of sky, but the gaze of
the Saints is so compelling that we have much less
difficulty in unifying the picture than in the Botticelli. Later in the Madonna Foligno of the same
gallery (Fig. 38), Raphael breaks the line between
the two worlds by placing the lower part of the
figure of the Madonna in the space between the
Saints. The hands of the figures in the lower part
of the picture are so well arranged that wherever
we glance the eye is guided to the Madonna. On
the left we follow the arms extended toward the
observer to the arm of St. John and then to the
Virgin; or if our eyes fall first on the right, they
turn directly to the Virgin as indicated by the
folded hands, or first to the Angel as directed by the

extended hand, and then with the Angel's gaze to the central figure. The direction of the eyes of the Saints and Angels is so well calculated to blend with the lines of the figures, especially with those of the arms, that the picture presents the most closely knit unity. Even if we glance first at the Virgin and Child, we shall be compelled to unite the two parts of the picture either by following the gaze of the Virgin down to the Saint, or that of the Child to the Angel. In the Disputa in the Vatican in Rome (Fig. 39), Raphael has painted a strip of sky which divides the two parts of the picture, but the clouds are curved toward the earth, which greatly aids the downward empathy if we gaze first at the upper part of the picture. In the lower part the figures are very cleverly arranged to guide the attention. In the center an arm conspicuously points to Christ in the clouds, and from both the right and left sides of the picture we are guided to the central point from figure to figure by extended arms and carefully grouped heads. The numerous figures in the clouds by similar arrangement complete the unity. In Titian's Assumption the strong empathic impulses upward most effectively unite the various parts of the picture. Guercino, a minor painter, has failed to realize the importance of the direction of line, in his St. Petronilla in the Palazzo dei Conservatori in Rome (Fig. 40). The figures engaged in the burial scene are all looking toward the bottom of the picture; the lines of the heavenly scene bind that part of the composition into a separate unit; consequently the observer must always make two distinct and unconnected adjustments in order to understand the picture.

In the pictures of the Madonna Enthroned a conventionalized scheme of unity has been employed. The Madonna is placed in the center of the picture with an equal number of Saints on either side. These figures direct the eye by gestures and gaze to the center of the picture, but some artists are cleverer than others in making use of these factors. Ghirlandaio, in his pictures in the Uffizi (Fig. 41) and the Academy in Florence (Fig. 42), has placed two of the kneeling figures conspicuously in the foreground as a guide, but he has caused confusion by arranging the other figures at different degrees of depth toward the rear. Most of the artists have avoided thus placing the figures. Some have bound the figures still closer together by the arrangement of the architectural background. For example, in the picture by a pupil of Botticelli in the Uffizi (Fig. 43) the figures are crowded into a sort of square alcove, formed by a high wall. In the picture by a pupil of Botticelli in the Academy in Florence (Fig. 44) each of his four Saints and the Madonna have panels behind them which themselves are strongly bound architecturally to one another, while in Botticelli's picture in the Kaiser Friedrich Museum in Berlin (Fig. 45) the plants or hedge at the back form three arches, one around each Saint and one around the

Virgin and Child.   In Filippino Lippi's picture in
the Uffizi (Fig. 46), not alone are the figures placed
in a small chapel, but Angels point to the Madonna
and thus prevent the gaze from wandering away
from the center to the ceiling.   In Raphael's Madonna of the Baldacchino in the Pitti (Fig. 47), the
same motive has been used.   The two pillars to the
extreme right and left guide the attention to the
roof.   Before our eyes reach it, they meet the Angels
who hover over the scene and point to the Virgin.
The two Saints, pillars, Angels, and canopy form a
square which completely confines the gaze.   The
attitude of the Saints at the sides of the picture
is typical of such a group.   One Saint is turned
toward the observer, inviting his gaze and directing it toward the center by a gesture; the other is
himself looking toward the center, and we follow
his gaze rather than his hand.

§ 2. Centering of Interest Through Objects Placed in the Foreground

Beside the above means of centering the interest,
artists have frequently placed objects in the center
of the lower part of the picture to attract attention
to the middle of the composition, such as a small
picture and urn at the foot of the throne in the
Berlin Botticelli (Fig. 45), a vase of flowers on the
rug covering the steps of the throne in the Ghirlandaio of the Uffizi (Fig. 41), a book placed with
seeming carelessness at the point of interest in the
Filippino Lippi (Fig. 46).   Often one or more cher-

ubs stand in the foreground at the foot of the throne or are seated on the steps, as in the Raphael picture in the Pitti, or are at the extreme bottom of the picture as in his Sistine Madonna in Dresden.

This method of directing attention is not distinctive of the groups of Madonna and Saints, but is frequently found in other compositions. In a picture by Paris Bordone of the Fisherman and the Doge in the Academy in Venice (Fig. 48), the boy in the foreground is leaning toward the priest and the attention is guided from him to the priest and then in a direct line to the fisherman and the Doge. In Titian's Visitation in the same gallery the old woman on the steps serves the same function as the boy in Bordone's picture. In all pictures where there are a great many figures, there would be much difficulty in perceiving the main features of the composition if it were not for such guiding objects.

§ 3. Binding Effect of Architectural Backgrounds

In the pictures previously described, mention was made of the binding effect of the architecture. In many pictures it is very obvious that the arches, pillars, and walls serve a purpose beyond that of a background for the main group. In the Annunciation by Andrea del Sarto, in the Pitti (Fig. 49), the arch of the building has not been thus placed by chance or even to balance the picture, but to connect the Angel with the Virgin. In the portrayal of this subject, we have a perpendicular division of the picture in two halves, which has troubled artists as much as the horizontal division between heaven and earth. Some have overcome the difficulty by having a scroll of words issuing from the Angel's mouth toward the Virgin, or by introducing the dove as a connecting link. Del Sarto was evidently weary of this symbolism and therefore painted in the background so that the eye is guided from the hand of the Angel to the pillar and around the curve of the arch to the Virgin. Although it is made evident by the size of the figure of the man on the steps that the building is not in the same plane with the Angel and Virgin, still the lines of pillar and arch very successfully unify the two halves of the picture. In Albertinelli's Visitation in the Uffizi (Fig. 50), there is not the same necessity for uniting the two figures, for they are drawn in the space of a triangle, and are also closely united by their embrace. Nevertheless, the same method of pillar and arch used by del Sarto is employed here to complete the union of the figures, and provide against the possibility that the attention will wander aimlessly among the clouds at the top of the picture. Domenichino's Communion of St. Jerome, in the Vatican Gallery (Fig. 51), also uses the architecture in this manner, and in order to make doubly sure that the eye will return from the top of the picture to the central figures, several Angels are arranged in a line which points to the dying Saint.

§ 4. Unity Through Suggested Movement

The arrangement of the figures in the shape of a triangle is the classical form of binding them, but many other shapes have been tried, such as the ellipse in Fra Angelico's picture of the Last Judgment in the Academy in Florence (Fig. 52) or the lunette of the Luca della Robbia plaque in the Bargello (Fig. 53), or the Madonna of the Sack of Andrea del Sarto in the Annunziata in Florence (Fig. 54). The skill of the artist was very severely taxed at times to place all his figures within the triangle, but the form acted as a safe guide for the maintenance of unity, although the figures had frequently to be placed in awkward positions in order to crowd them into the triangular shape, as may be observed in Fra Bartolommeo's Deposition in the Pitti (Fig. 55), or da Vinci's St. Ann, Virgin and Child in the Louvre, Paris (Fig. 56). A closer unity is hardly conceivable than that obtained in these latter pictures.

The stronger the empathic movement that the lines arouse in the observer, the closer will be the unity. The artist who is able to arouse strong empathic movements from one part of the picture to the other, does not need to resort to other methods of unification. For instance, in Michael Angelo's Creation of Man, on the ceiling of the Sistine Chapel (Fig. 57), through the dynamic value which is imparted to the lines of the arms of the two figures, one almost feels the spark of life leap from the fingers of God to those of Adam, and a perfect unity is produced in this way, in spite of the fact that there is a broad and bright strip of color between the two dark masses, and the lines of the two halves of the picture not only do not overlap but do not even touch at any point. In the Marriage of St. Catherine by Luini, in the Museum Poldi-Pezzoli in Milan (Fig. 58), on the other hand, there is much spatial unity produced by overlapping, but the empathic effect is weak and consequently the unity is not so strong as in the painting by Michael Angelo.

Some artists have attempted to portray several themes in the same picture, with the result that the mind is confused even though one of the scenes is made dominant and the others incidental. So strong is the distracting effect of the unconnected content that the formal elements of the picture are not able to achieve the unity necessary for a thorough enjoyment of it. A good example of this is the Filippo Lippi Virgin and Child in the Pitti (Fig. 59). In the foreground are the Virgin and Child, the beauty of which one desires to enjoy, but one's attention is distracted by a group of visitors on the right, by the birth scene of the Virgin on the left, and by the figures in the extreme background. It is impossible to unite these into one idea and the distraction is comparable to listening to a symphony when another orchestra is near by. Ghirlandaio's Birth of the Virgin in Sta. Maria Novella in Florence (Fig. 60) has a similar effect. The birth scene is prominent, but on the left is the visitation, and in the upper part of the picture is a frieze of small children whose animated movements in no way coincide with the arrangement of the rest of the picture. It must also be remembered that many of the figures are portraits of celebrated women of the time. Our attention is directed toward them by the grouping and the glances of the attendant, as well as to the Child by the act of the maid preparing the bath, so there is a very unpleasant conflict of empathic impulses in the very center of the picture. The distraction must have been still greater for the contemporaries of the artist, since there would have been the interest in the well-known society women. Time, by increasing the distance in the observer, has favored the unity in this respect. In Ghirlandaio's Birth of St. John the Baptist in Sta. Maria Novella in Florence (Fig. 61), the secondary scenes have been eliminated, and there is a centralization of interest in the Child, produced by the grouping and the outstretched hands of the figure on the left, but the attention is here also drawn toward the visitors, and the scene, which otherwise would have been one of delightful calm and dignity, is one of restlessness produced by the conflicting interests. This is a very good instance of what is constantly occurring in art, namely, that the artist is influenced by the conventions of his time, which either blind him to the essentials of beauty or, through their importance for his local reputation, make him indifferent to the more fundamental principles of his art. It cannot be said either that there were not excellent examples from the past for these artists to follow, such as Giotto's well-unified and dignified groupings.

The Adoration of the Magi has involved for most artists the handling of a great crowd, and some have cared little how the figures were arranged, so long as they were brought into the picture. There has been generally at least some arrangement of the figures about the central group, as in Filippino Lippi's picture in the Uffizi (Fig. 62), which has more of a decorative than a pictorial value. Gentile da Fabriano, in his picture in the Academy in Florence (Fig. 63), made the mistake, so far as unity is concerned, of turning the procession in the background away from the main scene, and not toward it, as Ghirlandaio did in his picture in the same gallery (Fig. 64). Leonardo da Vinci found that the portrayal of so many figures, no matter how well arranged, was distracting, and therefore disturbing to the beauty of the scene, so that, with characteristic independence of the customs of his age, he eliminated all but the most essential figures, although he was entirely capable of unifying a large group.

In the treatment of crowds, the greater the force in the suggested movement, provided the movement itself is unified, the more completely will the picture be apprehended as a whole. A comparison of the picture by Gentile Bellini of the Miracle of the Holy Cross in the Academy in Venice (Fig. 65) with Raphael's Heliodorus in the Vatican (Fig. 66), will make this principle clear.   In the former picture, the figures, which are well arranged about the central scene, are quietly standing or kneeling, and so passive are they and so indifferent to their neighbors that our attention is inclined to wander from group to group according to whim.   It is only through the fact that the onlookers are arranged in a ring about the central actors and are turned toward the miracle that the picture is held together. When we empathize in the various attitudes of the observers of the scene, we feel a lack of force. There is no leaning forward, no figures pointing, no intensity of gaze.   In fact, the figures are decidedly lackadaisical and seemingly devoid of any great interest in what is occurring.   In the Heliodorus, on the other hand, there is only one thing that we can do, for we are almost literally swept from figure to figure, beginning on the left, past the pointing group to the man on the pillar, and with all his intensity of attitude to the priest at the altar, and then with the violent movement of runners and horsemen to the recumbent figure on the right.   We experience little hesitancy anywhere. If we stop for a moment at the priest, the pointing women urge us on toward the horsemen.   If we fail at once to observe the priest on account of the movements on either side of the picture, the figure on the pillar soon attracts our attention in his direction.   Every line of force has a definite meaning

relative to the unity of the whole picture, and so
well coördinated are they that as soon as we have
perceived the various lines, the picture closes into
a compact form, a result which is difficult of attainment in such a composition, but when successful is one of the most satisfactory in art.   A picture
which, delightful in other respects, has failed in regard to unity is Carpaccio's St Jerome Leading
the Lion into the Monastery, in San Giorgio
degli Schiavoni in Venice (Fig. 67).   Carpaccio is an
artist who usually attains a large degree of unity,
but he has seldom dealt with such strong forces as
in this picture.   The monks in the foreground are
running precipitately toward the right, while
others in the background are fleeing with equal
haste toward the left; consequently one is pulled
in two directions at once with a result so painful
that the true merit of the picture suffers.

How strong are the various factors of unity
which have thus far been enumerated, is shown in
the picture by Bernardino Luini, of the Madonna
Addolorata and Christ with the Cross in the Museum Poldi-Pezzoli in Milan (Fig. 68).   Superficially
they are two pictures, for a pilaster of the frame
separates the Madonna from the Christ.   This is
hardly noticed, however; so closely bound together
are the figures by the Cross extending from Christ
to the Madonna, by the direction of gaze of the
two heads, and by the strong empathic effect of the
man's arm which, extending from the picture on the
right, violently pushes the shoulder of the Madonna

in an attempt to thrust her aside, but without effect, thus emphasizing in an unusually successful manner, through the unity, the strength of the devotion which is binding Mother and Son.

§ 5. Attraction of Attention Through Detailed Execution

A final form of centralizing the attention is a fundamental psychological one, and one which was first successfully employed by Velasquez—the founder of Impressionism. When we look at a landscape or a person, our eyes rest upon the chief point of interest. If it is a person, the attention will be directed to the face. This will then be clearly perceived, and so long as the eyes do not move, the rest of the figure will be seen with increasing indistinctness toward the outer field of vision. True to the direct impression made upon the mind, Velasquez has painted clearly the details of the face, but the design becomes more and more sketchy the farther it is from the central point. For example, the design in the lace about the collar is plainly indicated, as well as the pattern in the cloth of the dress, but the trimming about the sleeves will probably be found to be a single stroke of white paint, and often the pattern will entirely disappear toward the bottom of the garment. This effect may be seen in most of Velasquez's portraits and in those of most modern painters. A good example is the Infanta Margareta by Velasquez, in the Prado in Madrid (Fig. 69).

As a result of this treatment, the face stands out prominently, and the attention is fixed upon it while the indistinctness of the greater part of the picture is so in harmony with experience that one is in no way disturbed by it. On the contrary, it is a very welcome aid to the proper distribution of attention. In the perception of such a portrait, there is no wandering of the attention from point to point in the picture, but almost at once it is perceived as a whole, each factor in the composition having its proper effect.

In describing the unity of pictures, we have almost invariably mentioned a central point of interest and subordinate factors to right and left. Thus far, we have been concerned with the manner in which subordinate factors were related to one another, and to the point of greatest interest. We have not yet reached the end of our problem, however, for every means thus far enumerated for obtaining unity might be employed, but if the two halves of the picture do not balance each other, the composition will not be a success. Balance is absolutely necessary for unity in all the arts, and owing to its importance, a discussion of its nature, together with that of the principle of proportion, will form the subject of a separate chapter.

CHAPTER IX

BALANCE AND PROPORTION.

§ 1. BALANCE ABOUT THE PERPENDICULAR AXIS

A CHILD or a member of a primitive race, in arranging a composition, will almost invariably place the main figure in the center, with other objects frequently identical in shape equally distant on either side. For example, in drawing a house, the child tends to place the door in the middle and on either side a window and these of equal size. This gives a perfect symmetry, and is the simplest way of obtaining horizontal balance.[1] It is also the easiest balance for the observer to understand. Nevertheless symmetrical balance is rarely found in well-developed art. The balance is made asymmetrical in various ways, either by placing dissimilar objects on each side of the center or at different distances from it, by moving the point of balance or fulcrum off the center, or by both moving this point of balance and introducing objects of various shapes, sizes, and colors. The balance is thus made

[1] The *Century Dictionary* defines symmetrical as "The metrical correspondence of parts with reference to a median plane, each element of geometrical form having its counterpart upon the opposite side of that plane, in the same continued perpendicular to the plane, and at the same distance from it, so that the two halves are geometrically related as a body and its image in a plane mirror:" etc. Some authors include every form of balance under the term "symmetry," but the word is here used as defined above, and other forms of balance, where there is not this bilateral correspondence, are termed "asymmetrical balance."

increasingly complex.   In this balance there is involved the mechanical principle of the lever.   The
simplest form, that is in the æsthetic sense, corresponds to the mechanical balance where equal
weights are equally distant on either side of the
fulcrum or point of suspension.   If a heavy weight
is placed on one side of the fulcrum, a light weight
must be placed farther from the fulcrum on the
other side.

§ 2. FACTORS SUGGESTING WEIGHT.

In architecture and sculpture the principle of
balance according to mechanical laws, is readily
understood, but there are no "weights" in fine
arts, music, literature, and the drama.   We have
then to inquire what corresponds in these fields of
art to the weights in mechanical balance; that is,
what are the objective factors that must be considered by the artist in order to induce a sense of
balance, and what is the psychological equivalent
of this mechanical balance?   When this last is
answered, we shall know why we desire balance,
and in what way it is related to unity.   We shall
also be in a position to decide why certain forms of
balance and proportion are preferred.

It would be well to commence with some of the
factors used to produce balance, and the manner
of their arrangement.   An interesting study of
balance in the fine arts was made by Miss Puffer,[1]

---

[1] "Studies in Symmetry," *Harvard Psychological Studies*, Vol. I, pp. 467–
539.

and as the results throw considerable light upon
the problem, the experiment will be described in
some detail. Her first experiment was to determine in what relation to each other, upon a black
surface, we would place two vertical narrow white
strips of cardboard, one of which was twice as long
as the other, in order to obtain a pleasing balance.
One strip was placed at a certain distance from the
middle of the black background, and the other was
moved back and forth on the other side of the center until a balance was obtained. This was repeated for various positions of the stationary vertical strip. It was found that in many instances
the strips were arranged in imitation of mechanical
balance; that is, the smaller strip which was half
the size of the larger strip was placed twice as far
from the center. Exceptions occurred when both
lines would have had to be very near the center or
the edge; then the observer felt that the large
unoccupied spaces were disturbing, and he consequently deviated from the mechanical balance arrangement. It is probable that when the strips
were near the center or the edges, the observer
balanced each half of the surface independently
of the other half. At any rate, whatever the explanation, such instances are of value as showing
that many unsuspected factors may come in to determine æsthetic judgments.

The next experiment was upon the factor of
suggested movement. One of the strips was
pointed at the top, thus giving the direction of

movement, and inclined at an angle of 45 degrees. In one experiment it was turned toward the center, and in the other away from it. It was found that if the inclination of the strip was away from the center, the strip itself was brought nearer the center, but if the inclination was toward the center the strip was placed farther from the center. This means that a suggested movement out from the center produced a sense of lightness and *vice versa*.

Experiments were then made to determine the effect of what Miss Puffer termed "intrinsic interest," which she defines as "The interest which would attach to an object quite apart from its place in the space composition. In a picture it would be represented by the interest in an important person, in an unusual object, or in an especially beautiful object, if that beauty were independent of the other forms in the picture—as, for instance, a lovely face, or a jeweled goblet, etc." [1] Two postage stamps in black and white were placed on either side of the center, one of the stamps being changed from experiment to experiment in order to hold the interest, the other remaining the same. It was found that with few exceptions, the changed stamp, that is, the object possessing the greater interest, was placed nearer the center than the mechanical balance demanded, thus proving that interest acted like a mechanical weight.

[1] *Op. cit.*, pp. 499–500.

The final experiment was concerned with the effect of depth of vista. Two pictures, 80 mm. square, were used. The one was that of a railway tunnel, closed tightly at the entrance by a massive door. The other was of identical form and surroundings, but with the door open, showing the perspective of the rails, the blackness within the tunnel, and the small circle of light at the farther end. The observers were requested to "feel the third dimension as vividly as possible—to project themselves down the vistas, as it were—then to arrange the squares in the most pleasing manner." The picture which suggested a vista seemed to have the greater weight value, and was placed nearer the center. It was found later in analyzing classical pictures, that vistas were frequently used to obtain balance in the manner described. In such pictures the vista was opposed to other seemingly heavy elements, and the heavier these elements appeared the deeper was the vista used.

§ 3. Explanation of the Perception of Suggested Weight

The question why these various factors should balance under these conditions remains to be answered; that is, what is the underlying psychological explanation, for it is not sufficient to say that such factors have "weight." In many cases there is not the slightest intimation of actual weight in one's perception. Let us analyze the various experiences in order to discover if there is not ultimately one explanation applicable to them all, namely, the balance of motor impulses. This principle was accepted by Miss Puffer, but unfortunately she obscured it by referring ultimately to the function of attention. In the first place, we must remember that the principle of the perception of objects is, as has been set forth, motor adjustment toward that object, and when the perception is an æsthetic one there is an empathic adjustment in the object. In the experiment with the strips of unequal size, the larger strip may through experience suggest greater weight, and there will then be a stronger empathic response; that is, we shall feel a downward pull which will be greater on the side of the larger strip; unless, then, the laws of mechanical balance are observed, the composition will tilt toward that side and the experience will be unpleasant. It is not necessary that there be a conscious mental process of calculating how far out such a weight should be placed according to mechanical laws. In fact, it is probable that such a calculation is seldom made. We have frequently had the experience of balancing objects in this way, so that we soon get the "feel" of such a situation. It is quite possible that some persons can place the strip accurately according to this "feel" although they are unacquainted with the laws of mechanical balance. There are, indeed, many builders who know by the "feel" of things how to support their weights without being able to work the problem out on paper.

It is quite possible that in some instances the mechanical principle of the lever does not underlie an æsthetic balance. There may be merely a balancing of motor impulses on either side, in which case it would not be correct to speak of "weight." The balance will then consist of our empathy in the short perpendicular strip plus the empathic sweep through the longer distance to the center, which total strength of impulse will equal the empathy in the longer perpendicular strip plus the shorter sweep to the center. The most easily recognized balance of impulses is where motion is suggested by an object such as a horse galloping away from the center of the picture. Unless there is some compensating impulse in the opposite direction, the result will be disastrous so far as æsthetic enjoyment is concerned. The various forms of reaction, however, are not essentially different, for they all reduce to a balance of empathic responses. In that balance where the line inclines or points toward the center, there is a restriction of the empathy from the center to the object, so that the latter must be placed farther from the center than when the line is inclined away from the center. In the experiment with the vistas there is an increased empathic activity as soon as the observer imagines himself looking into the depth of the picture, or "plunging down the third dimension," according to Miss Puffer's description.[1]   Added to this the

[1] *Op. cit.*, p. 528.

perception of greater depth which involves that of more space may arouse the idea of weight. In any case, the vistas must, on account of this greater activity, be placed near the center or else be counterbalanced by some very strong element. In explanation of the increased "weight" of an object, which is constantly changed, it is not sufficient to speak merely of increased interest, because interest can be reduced to augmented motor responses, for that is what underlies the mental state called interest. Any object of beauty whatsoever, as soon as it arouses our interest, stimulates our empathic responses and these the artist must be careful to bring to some sort of balance.

Why brighter colors seem, as a rule, lighter in weight than darker colors is not so evident. Dr. Edgar Pierce, for example, found that the darker colors, blue, maroon, and green, are placed nearer the center in balancing than are the brighter colors, white, red, and orange.[1] There is probably even here a characteristic empathic response, a feeling of expansion or contraction perhaps, which influences the apparent weight of the colors. Undoubtedly the associations from previous experience with the colors are also important factors in balance. Even the setting in which the colors are placed makes a difference in the effect produced by them. Although one may say in general that white is lighter in weight than black, a white moon on a

[1] "Æsthetics of Simple Form," *Psychol. Rev.*, 1894, I, p. 494.

black background has been used to balance a large object on the other side of the picture.[1]

§ 4. Why Symmetry and Balance are Desired

That symmetry and balance are pleasing is acknowledged by all, but there is a difference of opinion regarding the cause of this pleasure. One theory has been that the feeling for symmetry has developed from that of usefulness. Utensils were made with two handles, one on either side, huts were built symmetrically, for practical reasons instruments had to be balanced, etc. Of how much influence this factor of usefulness was on the development in the race of the sense of symmetry is difficult to state, but there seems to be direct evidence from anthropological investigations that primitive people purposely changed their pictorial designs and their utensils in the direction of symmetry where not the slightest question of usefulness was involved. Representation of animals is the most usual form of primitive art. When they were drawn full-face, symmetry was easily obtained, but even when the animals were depicted in profile, the two eyes and other symmetrical features were represented. One can also readily

---

[1] There are various other means of obtaining balance, some of which have been described by Dr. Denman Ross. He speaks for example of the balance of motion and weight: "It will sometimes happen, that a gradation of tones or measures will draw the eye in a certain direction, toward the greater contrast, while a larger mass or measure of tone, on the other side, will be holding it back. In such a case we may have a mass balancing a motion." *A Theory of Pure Design*, p. 178.

trace, through a series of primitive designs, the development from a recognizable though conventional representation of an animal, to the symmetrical pattern which has lost almost all resemblance to the original.[1] Also we find that the same primitive people may show the greatest irregularity when their drawings are to serve a practical purpose, but that the designs become symmetrical as soon as they are used for decorative purposes, as in tattooing. The symmetry of many of the designs, most of them being conventional representations of living creatures, shows a high degree of ingenuity on the part of primitive artists.

These facts make it very probable that the desire for symmetry and other forms of balance is a distinct and independent one, and not a chance development. If this is true, it is necessary to know why balance is found to be not only pleasing but necessary where we have art form. Even those who believe in inherited forms of response could hardly be satisfied with the explanation that it was an original instinct. We must therefore seek the solution in experience. The most obvious one has seemed to be that symmetry appeals because man himself is symmetrically built. If we accepted this it would still be necessary to explain why man should desire art to be always shaped according to his own image, why he would not rather tire of such a construction and desire a new one. There is also the fact that it is a very rare exception for man to

[1] E. D. Puffer, *Studies in Symmetry*, p. 475.

be built symmetrically. He is almost invariably larger on one side than on the other, and there are all sorts of irregularities in the human figure. No matter how he is constructed, however, there is one thing he finds it necessary to maintain, and that is physical balance. Anything which disturbs his equilibrium he necessarily finds disagreeable, and the maintenance of balance has through practice become one of his most firmly established habits. If the body tilts to one side, there is an instant response from antagonistic muscles to restore the balance. It is fair to assume then that a balance of motor impulses and an equalizing of the accompanying feelings of strain,[1] no matter what muscle groups may be involved, soon become a well-established desire of the organism. If to this we add the habit of empathic response, we shall have at least a plausible theory to explain the desire for balance in art.

Lotze, with his usual clear insight, has offered an explanation of symmetry which is in entire accord with the findings of modern psychology. He has written: "I am certain that the investigator can convince himself that the agreeableness of spatial symmetry does not depend directly upon the regularity of proportional relations [in the object], but rather indirectly upon the pleasantness which

---

[1] For a description of the physiological processes, that is, "the corresponding equality of muscular innervations involved," see "Æsthetics of Unequal Division," by R. P. Angier, *Harvard Psychological Studies*, Volume I, pp. 550–551.

is occasioned by the perception of the movement [in ourselves]." [1] He further says that the mere mathematical formula leaves us cold; that it is not the identity of the parts, but the balance which is æsthetically operative, and as we cannot speak of balance unless we are acquainted with weight and the forces by which objects are moved in space, so it is this experience which must be in the consciousness of all those who believe that they derive æsthetic pleasure from purely geometrical relations. "We can understand these mechanical relations æsthetically only in so far as we can feel ourselves into the particular weal and woe which moving things experience through their motion, and those in equilibrium through their repose, and for this experience the coöperation of our organism, instead of being a distracting factor, is, indeed, essential." [2]

---

[1] *Geschichte der Æsthetik*, p. 76.

[2] *Ibid.*, pp. 78–79. It will be recognized that Lotze is describing a process of empathy. In fact, he was among the first to call attention to it, and to the importance of bodily processes in general, to perception. A few pages farther on, he describes more fully what he means by empathic response. The passage is taken entirely from his *Mikrokosmus*, where it is stated that "We not only contract our sensitive mental tendrils into as small a space as possible in order to share the dreams of the restricted existence of the mussel and the monotonous delight of its opening and shutting reactions, we not only expand into the slender forms of the trees whose branches are animated by the breeze into graceful bendings and swayings; we even transfer these interpretive feelings into the inanimate, thus enabling us to transform the dead weight and support of buildings into so many limbs of a living organism whose inner tensions pass over into ourselves." (Vol. II, Book 5, Chap. 2, p. 202.) In the *Geschichte*, Lotze is describing Herder's æsthetic principles, but he says that Herder did not state the above view with the exactitude with which he, Lotze, has given it to us, although it was dis-

A design which has a heavier object on one side of the center than on the other, or whose lines suggest greater activity or movement on one side will arouse in us a greater response on that side. This response, however, will appear to be expressed in the design itself, thus giving it a tendency to incline to one side or to fly apart, or in the case of lack of perpendicular balance, to tip over. That is, it will seem to lack stability, and the unity of the picture will be disturbed. Artists who have not carefully studied composition or analyzed their own reactions sometimes "feel" that there is something wrong with the arrangement of their design, that it is restless and lacks that coherence which unity demands, without their being able to determine the cause. It also happens that some artists do not respond to any great extent to form and balance; that is, they lack the sensitiveness necessary for correct composition. It may be that their interests are almost entirely absorbed by some other feature of the work such as color, or because their only desire in beauty is to represent their model. If so, the form and balance hardly enter their consciousness, and consequently their pro-

tinctly Herder's endeavor to show that objects of beauty are not merely vaguely suggestive but expressive. It is fair to assume, however, that credit for the psychological principles expressed belonged to Lotze and not to Herder. See also Fechner's remarks upon Lotze's theory; "Zur Experimentalen Æsthetik," Abhandlungen der Sächsischen Gesellschaft der Wissenschaften, *Mathem. Phys. Classe* IX, p. 565. Fechner saw nothing in Lotze's view but an insistence upon association factors and failed to grasp the deeper significance of his theory not only for æsthetics but for all perception.

ductions never receive the highest approval.   An
instance might be cited of an artist who had
painted a seascape, which showed a delightful harmony of color—the gray of the fog, the green of the
water, and a touch of brighter color in the sail.
The composition was expressive of the mystery of
the sea, but the artist realized that something was
wrong.   Although there was a dead calm at sea
and the sail-boats were moving slowly, one felt a
strange uneasiness for which one was able to account by the fact that the two ships in the picture
were moving in opposite directions, thus making it
appear as if the picture were being pulled apart.
Not only was this disturbing in itself, but it was
also totally out of harmony with the spirit of the
composition.   There was a balance of masses to
which factor the artist was duly sensitive, but not
a balance of suggested movement.   As Dr. Denman
Ross has said in a similar connection: "The balance
of inclinations is felt more than the balance of
shapes." [1]

Not every one is able to describe his empathic
reactions as accurately as Miss C. Anstruther-
Thomson has done, but one will probably recognize
in her account something of one's own experience.
In describing her æsthetic appreciation of a jar,
she writes: "To begin with, the feet press on the
ground while the eyes fix the base of the jar.   Then
one accompanies the *lift up*, so to speak, of the body
of the jar by a *lift up* of one's own body; and one

[1] *A Theory of Pure Design*, p. 87.

accompanies by a slight sense of downward pressure of the head the downward pressure of the widened rim on the jar's top. . . . Moreover, the shape of the jar provokes movements of balance, the left curve a shifting on to the left foot, and *vice versa*. A complete and equally distributed set of bodily adjustments has accompanied the ocular sight of the jar; this *totality* of movements and *harmony* of movements in ourselves answers to the intellectual fact of finding that the jar is a *harmonious whole*." [1] It would have been more accurate to state that the harmony of movement in ourselves *is* the intellectual fact.

A lack of symmetry in design may even seem to affect the breathing, according to Miss Anstruther-Thomson, possibly through a contraction of the muscles on the one side. This is mentioned here to show that the balance may be not only between muscles directly concerned with equilibrium, although it is very probable that they are the most frequently involved, and are primarily the cause of our pleasure in balance. In describing her reaction to the so-called "honeysuckle pattern" of a Greek vase, she says: "As the eyes move upwards along the pattern, the two lungs draw in a long breath, and there comes a slight sensation of the sides of the thorax being stretched: this sensation of width continues while the breath moves upwards giving us simultaneously the sense of bilateral width and of height, the proportion between which being

[1] *Beauty and Ugliness*, pp. 175–176.

very pleasant to breathe, accounts for a sense of well-being while looking at the pattern. If we try to reproduce these sensations of harmony while looking at the *irregular shapes* in the room, we are met by impossibilities; we can no longer breathe equally on both sides, . . . " [1] To most readers such a reaction will seem very unnatural, and it will be objected that one is not conscious of such bodily reactions while enjoying the balance of a design. Such a criticsm is to some extent justified. Normally we are entirely unconscious of such movements in ourselves, as was stated when the process of empathy was described. What we experience is the result of these processes in the quality of the object perceived. It is only when we are set to examine our own bodily reactions that we notice them, but the fact that we are not explicitly aware of them does not mean that they are not operative in æsthetic appreciation. On the other hand, if we were constantly cognizant of them as in the previous description, we should lose much if not all of our joy in beauty.[2]

[1] *Op. cit.*, p. 186.
[2] The muscles of most individuals are stronger on one side of the body than the other, according as they are right or left handed. That being the case, it might be suggested that if the theory of balance depended upon the empathic response then the right-handed individuals would desire the heavier factors on the right side, and vice versa. Experiments have been made to determine whether there is a difference in preference between right- and left-handed individuals. Some indications of such differences have been found, but the results are not conclusive. Why should such inequality of strength, however, influence the æsthetic judgment of the individual? If he is weaker on one side, he has become accustomed to make a greater effort on that side to maintain his balance.

§ 5. Balance about the Horizontal Axis.

The balance about the horizontal axis is not the same as that about the perpendicular. While in the latter, we desire an equal distribution of "weight" to the right and left, in the former, we must have more "weight," more suggestion for response in the lower half of the picture than in the upper. In general the larger objects and the heavier colors are placed at the bottom of the composition. A design in the form of an inverted pyramid would be unpleasant unless further elaboration of the composition made it clear that the pyramid was supported in its position. Exceptions can be found to this simple rule of perpendicular balance, but some compensating factors are then necessarily present. For instance, there may be floating clouds or a flock of birds at the top of the picture, with little weight at the bottom. The fact, however, that the clouds are floating, that the birds are flying, arouses in us the sense of their being supported, and inhibits the downward thrust of weight.[1] Artists have even been able to fill the top of their canvas with dark heavy masses of clouds, which grow lighter as they approach the horizon, but it will be noticed that the vault of the heavens with its idea of support has been cleverly represented by the subtle gradation in the intensity of the colors. The clouds then become a roof and one feels the architectural aspect of the composition.

[1] See Kate Gordon, *Æsthetics*, p. 189.

Regarding perpendicular balance, Dr. Edgar Pierce has written: "The bottom was always of a different value from the top, and symmetry evidently played a very subordinate part. The principle here seems to be that of stability; the distances between the lines here suggests the idea of masses, and the effect must be stable, and not seem as if it were going to topple over." [1] The only objection to this statement is in the suggestion that there is a fundamentally different principle here from that operative in horizontal balance. Certainly stability is the quality that is desired in the perpendicular arrangement of masses, but it is also the underlying principle in horizontal balance. The difference lies in the manner in which it is attained; in a word, whether it is by the horizontal or the perpendicular distribution of the elements of the composition. In the last analysis it is the stability of the organism which must be considered, since that is one of the essentials to the unity of the perception and the beauty of the object.

There is an optical illusion that should be mentioned in this connection, for it greatly aids the perpendicular balance. If one is asked to bisect a perpendicular line without measuring it, one almost invariably places the mark too high. If a line is actually bisected, it is with difficulty that one can convince oneself that the upper half is not longer than the lower half. If, therefore, in design we place similar objects below and above the exact

[1] *Æsthetics of Simple Form*, p. 487.

middle in a desire for perpendicular symmetry, there will seem to be a greater concentration in the lower half, and thus greater stability, for there will be the same number of objects in a seemingly smaller space. The generally accepted explanation for this illusion is that there is an increasing strain in the eye muscles in looking toward the top of the picture. This increase in effort is perceived as an increase in distance traveled, if one is concerned with the subjective aspect of the eye movement, or in increased size of the object, if the sensations from the eye are unconsciously fused with the perception of the object.

§ 6. THE GOLDEN SECTION

In the horizontal balance we have seen that it is not necessary to place the dividing line exactly in the middle, so long as the balance is maintained. It has, therefore, been a problem of æsthetics to determine just where the division should be made in order to have the most pleasing effect for the majority of individuals. That bisection, while not unpleasant, does not entirely satisfy most observers, will be generally admitted. The division which has caused the most discussion is known as the "golden section," which is the proportion wherein the smaller section bears the same relation to the larger section that the larger does to the whole line. Roughly speaking, it is a proportion of 5:8::8:13. In a line thirteen inches in length, the golden section would be approximately five

inches from one end. Zeising found this ratio
pleasing because it expressed a harmonious unity
in multiplicity.[1]

Theodor Fechner [2] discussed this proportion at
some length and although he agreed that it was
pleasant, he criticised Zeising's [3] wide application
of the principle to the human figure, the leaves of
plants, the forms of crystal, the arrangements of the
planets, the proportions in architecture and statuary, and the relations of musical tones. Later, he
made the experiment of presenting parallelograms
of equal areas but different proportions, including
the square and the proportion of the golden section,
to over three hundred and fifty men and women,
and he found that about thirty-five per cent of
them chose the golden section, which was the highest percentage of any figure. The proportions that
were closest to the golden section had the next
highest percentage.[4] These experiments have a
very important historical value in that they mark
the first attempt to discover æsthetic principles by
means of scientifically controlled experimental
methods. Mention of the pleasing effect of this
division has been made in most books upon psychology and æsthetics. Further experiments were
conducted by other investigators to determine the
validity of Fechner's results, and it was found

[1] *Æsthetische Forschungen*, 1855, p. 172; also *Neue Lehre von den Proportionen des Menschlichen Körpers*, 1854, pp. 146–147.

[2] *Zur Experimentalen Æsthetik*, pp. 567–568.

[3] *Das Normalverhältniss der Chemischen und Morphologischen Proportionen.*

[4] *Vorschule der Æsthetik*, pp. 194 *et seq.*

that the golden section was not chosen in the majority of cases.[1] That the average of the judgments came near the golden section has no bearing upon the question, as Professor Angier rightly stated, for that is equivalent to saying that if green is chosen by some and blue by others, then green-blue is the most pleasing color.[2] What the experiments did substantiate, however, was the general tendency to choose some definite *asymmetrical* division, and the fact that the exact location differed among the individuals tested, although very few disliked the golden section, and most preferred a division which approximates it, so that Professor Witmer is, therefore, correct in his statement that "It seems to be true that the development of taste leads to a preference of proportion to symmetry, . . . But the cause of this is not the demand for an equality of ratios, but a demand merely for greater variety. Symmetrical figures are divided into parts monotonously alike; proportional figures have their parts unlike. The amount of unlikeness or variety that is pleasing will depend upon the general character of the object, and upon the individual's grade of intelligence and æsthetic taste. The ratio of 'proportion' is not fixed as is that of symmetry. It is only as a very rough approximation that the ratio of 3:5 can be said to

[1] See Lightner Witmer, "Zur Experimentalen Æsthetik Einfacher Räumlicher Form Verhältnisse," *Phil. Studien*, 1893, Vol. IX; and R. P. Angier, *The Æsthetics of Unequal Division.*
[2] See Valentine, *Experimental Psychology of Beauty*, p. 55.

represent the most pleasing mean between a too great inequality or variety and a too great equality or sameness." [1] Almost all writers have agreed that there is a desire for greater variety than is presented by symmetry, but those who have upheld the golden section as a canon of art cannot admit an approximation for they are for the most part influenced by the Pythagorean delight in the mathematical relation and unless the relation is an exact one, it can have no meaning for them. Zeising [2] is a typical example. He is particularly interested in the fact that in the golden section the relation between the whole and its parts is the same relation as that between the parts themselves. In this ratio, therefore, we are made aware of unity in the midst of difference. The whole is not a "dead sum" of equal parts but a "living product" of two unequal factors, and it is this union of these unequal factors which is the source of the beauty of the golden section.

This pleasure in purely abstract numerical relations has been one of the incentives for seeking standard proportions in art forms, such as the relations which Mr. J. Hambidge [3] has found to be fundamental in classic art. Such proportions are interesting to the student of the history of art, and perhaps of practical value in design and architecture, but the æsthetician gains very little from a

---

[1] *Analytical Psychology*, p. 74.

[2] *Neue Lehre von den Proportionen des Menschlichen Körpers*, p. 154.

[3] *Dynamic Symmetry, A Series of Practice Diagrams with Text.*

knowledge of these relations. That we have grown
accustomed to these particular proportions in nature is not a sufficient explanation for their use,
since these are only a few out of the infinite number
of such relations, nor are we aware even subconsciously of these numerical proportions. What
naïve observer, for instance, in viewing a line divided according to the golden section, has sufficient
clue to the relation of the parts to the whole line
that, as has been maintained, "The mental transfer
from attention to the whole line to attention to the
greater part, prepares us for the further transition
to the smaller part, because the step is proportion-
ally the same"?[1] In order to justify such a theory
it is necessary to resort to the hypothesis of unconscious counting, which is, to say the least,
highly problematical.

It is more than likely that the proportions
found by Mr. Hambidge were used by the Greeks
partly because of the pleasure in the logical development of one form from another, and partly because of the ease with which these forms could be
constructed.

§ 7. Preference for Asymmetrical Balance

Though the importance of these proportions
must be admitted, there is little satisfaction for the
æsthetician in the knowledge that the corner column of the Parthenon was placed in a particular
division of the total surface. What we desire to

[1] Valentine, *op. cit.*, p. 54.

know is why it was placed in that division rather than another. In other words, what æsthetic "feeling" prompted the Greeks to place it just where they did? It is not then a possibly definite ratio that seems important, but the reason why an asymmetrical division of a simple line or the relation of two lines or surfaces in a ratio other than that of 1:1 should be pleasing at all.[1]

The experiments of Professor Angier have shown that the same balance of motor impulses is obtained in perceiving a pleasant division of a simple line that occurs when there is direct suggestion of weight or movement: ". . . the center of interest is the division point, whence eye-movements, or innervations involving, perhaps, the whole motor system, are made to either side . . . the long section of the line gives a free sweep of the eyes from the division point, the center, to the end; or again, a free innervation of the motor system . . . then, with that as standard, the æsthetic impulse is to secure an equal and similar movement, from the center, in the opposite direction." [2] Such a description must be considered an account of the manner in which the total experience has influenced the perception and not of what goes on consciously in the mind whenever we have the impression of the pleasantness of such a division. That is, through such an experience as is described by Professor

[1] Probably the most important of Mr. Hambidge's contributions is his emphasis of the relations of surfaces rather than lines.

[2] *The Æsthetics of Unequal Division*, pp. 559–560

Angier, the organism assumes a definite set or form of reaction, which becomes entirely spontaneous.

What the reactions are which underlie our pleasure in certain proportions represented in figures such as the rectangle, is less obvious than in simple line division, but it is probable that similar factors of muscular balance are operative. It is true, however, that when we look at such a figure our pleasure seems immediate and we would deny that there is any conscious comparison of the height with the breadth. We seem to feel an instinctive liking for the figure. In the line division, we usually have to estimate and compare the length of the two sections before we come to a decision, but in the proportion of figures there is seldom evidence of such a process. Nevertheless, we do perceive the sides of a figure even if we are unaware of a comparison, and from what psychology teaches us of such a situation, it seems very possible that an unconscious motor adjustment is initiated by the lines, a definite and as a rule spontaneous set which has as its basis a balance of impulses. A certain proof of the validity of this assumption seems to lie in the fact that when we are uncertain whether or not we like the proportion, we move our eyes up and down and across the surface.

More convincing than laboratory experiments is the fact that an asymmetrical balance, especially one which approximates the golden section, is admitted by most artists to be in general, a desirable proportion. One famous modern portraitist has even had a pocket instrument made to enable him readily to identify the golden section. Some have expected to find that exact golden section ratio in all pleasing proportions, but this has not been verified. There is indeed a great danger in such matters of finding what one desires.[1] If, however, we examine pictures which are usually considered pleasing, we shall notice that if the main figure is not in the center it is usually very close to the dividing point of the golden section. One hesitates to generalize, but it is probable that we shall find this to be the case in the majority of the compositions of to-day and in many of those of the old masters which have asymmetrical proportions, as for example, the portrait by a pupil of Botticelli (Fig. 27) and the portrait by Velasquez (Fig. 69). In the Madonna groups, tradition has for the most part

---

[1] How arbitrary such measurements are has been shown by Fechner in his *Zur Experimentalen Æsthetik*, pp. 572–575, and as every age seems to produce at least one disciple of Pythagoras it appears in place to summarize Fechner's remarks: An investigator by the name of Wolfe thought that the ratio of 1:1 could be shown to be a fundamental relation. He attempted to prove that this relation holds between the distance separating the Greek columns and their height. If he did not find it between every second column, he found it between every third, and if the proportion was not obtained by taking the distance from the middle of the column, then it was calculated from the middle of one column to the edge of the other, and if there was still a discrepancy then he added the height of the entablature to the pillar. He found that the human body was divided into two equal parts by placing the line at the junction of leg and thigh. Zeising by placing the dividing line at the navel, obtained his golden section proportion. Wolfe found that the head was divided into two equal parts by the horizontal line at the corner of the eyes, while Zeising found that the line from the top of the head to the middle of the neck was divided at the eyebrows, according to the golden section.

prescribed that the main figure shall be in the center. In fact, this is true in most of the religious pictures which have been mentioned, although the two halves are not symmetrical in design. Pleasing exceptions, however, may be observed, as in the Descent from the Cross by Bartolommeo, (Fig. 55) and the Visitation by Albertinelli (Fig. 50), where the chief point of interest is very close to the golden section.

In the development of architecture from the regular form of the Greek Cross to the form of the Gothic Cathedral, where the transept divides the nave from the choir close to the golden section, one can clearly see the desire for asymmetry. Professor Witmer has pointed out a similar change in the shape of the cross: "The cross was originally T-shaped, or had the cross-bar very high up on the vertical. In early forms of the cross . . . the cross-bar has a higher position than it occupies . . . on an ecclesiastical cross of the fifteenth century. As the historic symbol was adapted for church and personal ornament, the cross-bar dropped down in the course of centuries to satisfy an æsthetic demand for proportion in the vertical line." [1] The last statement is important in that it calls attention to the fact that such a change can occur from purely æsthetic reasons without any evident practical purpose, merely, as we should say, because the organism has found it more pleasant to adjust itself to such a form.

[1] *Analytical Psychology* p. 74.

§ 8. THE MOST PLEASING PROPORTIONS

For most of the investigators of proportion, the motive has been to find the most "perfect" relation, and many have gone so far as to prescribe such a proportion as the golden section for all objects that claim the attribute of beauty, but as was stated in a previous chapter, æsthetics cannot lay down fixed rules which must be followed under all circumstances. The most that can be said is that a given proportion will generally be found to be pleasing, but whether it should be used depends entirely upon the content which is to be expressed, or the quality of the emotion that is to be aroused. It may be a pleasing proportion for the frame of a picture or the shape of a house, but it would be truly absurd to demand that all frames and all houses should have such proportions. The same may be said of the proportions of the human figure. Throughout the ages, artists and æstheticians have been eager to find the perfect male and female figures, and because the Greek statues have received unusual favor, their proportions were carefully studied and frequently the relation of the golden section or some other more or less constant relation has been found.

It seems more to the point, however, as an explanation of their beauty, that they express by their lines perfect health and strength, the two qualities of the human form most desired by the race. We judge that they do express these attributes from the facts of our own experience. They are not too stout or too thin, too weak or too highly developed muscularly; that is, they do not show extremes, a fact which has led to the theory that they are pleasing because they represent the "mean" or the type. This may be true, but why should the type in itself be pleasing? Surely not because it represents the general idea of man, as some idealistic philosophers would have us believe, but because we know (and this, again, from experience) that such a type is the best equipped for all-round adaptation to the environment. That is what is most frequently desired, and when we empathize in such a form, we have the pleasure of feeling that that is true. The proportion carries out this idea, and in the talent of the artist in thus unifying this form of expression with his idea, lies the essence of the beauty of his work. But though this idea may be pleasing to most persons, it is not the only one sought in the human form, as any superficial study of art development reveals. Dürer spent years in the search for the ideal female form, and his women for the most part express the idea of fecundity. In Rubens' women, we find the acme of corpulence and indolence, with the associated ideas of rich food, a comfortable ménage, and a full purse. Botticelli's women on the other hand, are tall and thin—qualities suggestive of lightness and spirituality, as are also El Greco's men to an exaggerated degree. The artists were at the time possessed of a certain idea and had to express it.   We may not share their ideals, but we can nevertheless enjoy the perfection with which they express them in their proportions, as well as in their lines and colors.

Similar changes of proportion to suit a prevailing idea may be seen in styles of clothing.   There is the age of the hoop-skirt where the movements of the limbs are concealed, and the age of the hobble-skirt with its slimness of figure and restriction of movement.   One year the coats of men's attire have broad shoulders and narrow waists indicative of the athlete.   The next year, narrow shoulders and straight lines suggest the more intellectual and æsthetic type.   The change is in general due to our dislike of monotony and to the financial considerations of the tailor.   The ideas expressed follow sometimes from national conditions such as war, or renewed interest in athletics or art; more frequently, as it would seem, they are due to whimsies of the trade.   But, whatever may be the cause, we soon through suggestion accept the ideas which underlie the form of expression, and find the latter pleasing in its proportions unless we are able sufficiently to free ourselves from the prevailing idea and view the situation in the abstract.   We are then struck with such absurdities as a two-foot feather in the hat of the small woman to give her height, or as the shoulders of the thin young man padded some inches beyond his body to give him a muscular appearance.

That we must consider the effect desired in de-

termining the proportions to be used is readily seen
in architecture. Although the square form is almost always disagreeable, and the golden section
a safe venture, the latter gives a spaciousness to
the idea of the house as a whole or to the separate
rooms, which may be out of keeping with the temperament of the tenant. A low ceiling, or long and
narrow room, while usually oppressively contracting and restricting, expresses for some persons a
certain coziness, or if similar proportions are used
in the exterior outline of the house, there is, perhaps,
a blending with the surrounding scenery, which is for
some highly desirable. If we find the proportions of
our dwellings entirely satisfactory, it is because they
are in harmony with our predominating modes of
response, or what is the same thing in other terms,
because the proportions express our personality.

§ 9. Explanation of the Preference for Asym- metrical Balance

The final problem which remains to be solved is
that seeming preference for asymmetrical balance,
which was described at the beginning of the chapter. Even though such preference is not universal,
there is still the question why any one should
choose asymmetry when symmetrical arrangement
offers the easiest guide to motor balance of the
organism. The usual answer is that the mind desires variety. Most observers find it uninteresting
to unify a work of art by merely balancing off
against each other two opposite and nearly iden-

tical halves. It is like perceiving the repetition of the same object—we soon become adjusted to it and the continued repetition not only eventually robs it of all interest for us, but also robs it of its meaning, as, for example, the repetition of the same word until it becomes mere sound. If, for any reason, we are compelled long to endure such a monotonous repetition of sound, we become painfully disturbed; the entire organism seems to rebel. Dr. Santayana has written: "The tendency of monotony is double, and in two directions deadens our pleasure. When the repeated impressions are acute, and cannot be forgotten in their endless repetition, their monotony becomes painful. The constant appeal to the same sense, the constant requirement of the same reaction, tires the system, and we long for change as for a relief. If the repeated stimulations are not very acute, we soon become unconscious of them; like the ticking of the clock, they become merely a factor in our bodily tone, a cause, as the case may be, of a diffused pleasure or unrest; but they cease to present a distinguishable object." [1] To a certain degree our interest increases with increased difficulty of adjustment. As soon as our adaptation is perfected we seek a new one. There is a demand for activity, an ever-increasing activity. New problems are sought, new difficulties of balance desired. It is the same principle that we found in imagination and the unity of heterogeneous parts. It is true that to explain a de-

[1] *The Sense of Beauty*, pp. 106–107.

sire for change by the demand for greater activity
does not tell us why we have such a desire. A possible explanation of this is found in the necessity
of adjusting ourselves to an environment that
would otherwise overwhelm us. We learn by experience that we are surrounded by objects of increasing complexity. We also learn that it is
necessary to perfect our modes of response to them
not only for the present but for future situations.
The simpler adjustments are naturally first made,
and then by necessity we are urged to more complex ones. Pleasure is aroused by the results and
the process of adjustment soon becomes a pleasure
in itself and is welcomed in art as well as in the
more practical fields of man's endeavor. This opportunity that art gives for a more perfect adjustment of balance is another proof of the benefit
that we derive from the experience of beauty.

Such an explanation of the desire for asymmetry
is speculative, but it has a certain basis in the general development of balance from the simple to
the complex. Just how much asymmetry is found
to be pleasing, that is in itself and divorced from
content, depends upon the organism and its experience. A line which is bisected very near the
center is generally considered unpleasant because
it seems like a slight error in the attempt to obtain
symmetry. The desire for a proportion approx-
imating the golden section is probably due to the
fact that although we desire multiplicity, that
which the golden section offers taxes the adjust-

ment of the ordinary organism to its limit; although there are those who delight in going beyond this division almost to the end of the line.

An interesting develop-
ment is taking place at
present in the art educa-
tion of children. Not only
is much attention being
given to color and line, but
also to balance. Since children when left to them-
selves generally begin with
symmetry it was formerly
thought that they could
understand only this form
of design, so that they
were given stupidly sym-
metrical forms instead of
being introduced as soon
as possible to easy prob-
lems of asymmetry. Fig-
ure 70 is a delightful example of the sort of design
that children are now be-
ing asked to copy.[1] In all
but one respect it is symmetrical but the child is
shown that entire symme-

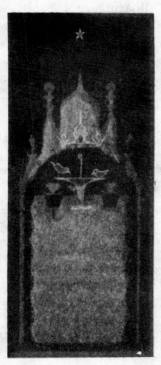

Fɪɢ. 70

Reproduced by permission of
Atkinson, Mentzer & Com-
pany, from the Industrial
and Applied Art Books.

try is not necessary; on the contrary, that a more

[1] *Industrial and Applied Art Books,* edited by E. E. and F. R. Bush,
Book IV, p. 7.

pleasing or subtle effect is obtained if there is slight variation. One of the birds is larger than the other and higher in the picture, but as it is floating in the air, we feel a certain lightness so that its actually greater weight is nicely balanced by the smaller bird seated on the fountain. The balance is so cleverly obtained that we shall probably not notice at first glance that there is not perfect symmetry, although we shall have the pleasure of the arrangement. Still more asymmetrical designs can be presented at successive stages until the child learns all the possibilities of balance and is able to feel and imitate the different effects.

What has been said concerning balance and symmetry in the visual arts, may be applied also to the other fields. If we admit the underlying balance of organic processes, it is not by way of mere analogy that we speak of the balance in literary productions and in the drama. Frequent mention has been made in æsthetic studies of the balance in the various scenes of the drama, that is, the opposition of conflicting forces that is continually presented as a play develops. But there is a more fundamental balance than this constant swing of the pendulum back and forth in equalizing phases, and that is the balance of the play as a whole. The plot is slowly unfolded, the dramatic incidents gather strength, and the strain of the audience increases until the crisis is reached. Then in a quick succession of incidents the resolution is accomplished.

Into the small space of the concluding scene are crowded a series of emotions which, if the play is to be successful, should equal in intensity the slow summation of the responses to the preceding acts. If there is not this balance, the audience is left unsatisfied. No matter how convincing the final answer of the problem may be, no matter how well the story itself may have been brought to a happy or tragic conclusion, the complete æsthetic pleasure will be absent if the tensions induced before the crisis are not matched by an equal amount of excitement in the release. A lack of balance of the structural elements of the drama would be as irrational as inconsistency in the plot. The audience demands to know why it has been induced to labor up to the height of the crisis and the only satisfactory answer that can be given is in an equal though swifter descent. Further, is it not more than a mere analogy that we prefer in the dramatic an asymmetrical balance, and that the balance most frequently found seems to approximate the proportions of the golden section? The crisis usually lies approximately three-fifths of the distance from the beginning of the play. We can visualize the situation by imaging the slow climb up the gradual slope of a hill and the quick descent on the other side to the original level. How intolerable a symmetrical drama would be; how impossible is even the conception of a play with the crisis in the middle, with equal slopes on either side. On the other hand, just as in the division of a line, under certain circumstances, the dividing line may be placed near one end, so the crisis can be placed near the close, if by a *tour de force* sufficient dramatic tension is crowded into the remaining moments.

CHAPTER X

ILLUSTRATIONS OF BALANCE FROM THE FINE ARTS

A FEW illustrations of the various forms of balance will be given from the pictures already used in the previous chapters. Except in some decorative designs, perfect symmetry is seldom found. The nearest approach is in those pictures where the main figure is in the center with an equal grouping on either side, such as the conventional pictures of the Madonna Enthroned; but the figures themselves are different and the Child is always held on one side of the center and must therefore be balanced in some way. For instance, Raphael's Madonna of the Baldacchino (Fig. 47) is almost symmetrical in line, but the Child, being to the left, is balanced on the right by the end figure, which being full face attracts more interest than does the figure on the opposite side. Again in the Ghirlandaio (Fig. 42) there is a symmetrical distribution of figures, but as the Child is to the left of the center, the figure in the right foreground is farther from the center than is its balancing figure. In his Madonna and Saints (Fig. 41), the balance is even more subtly attained. The figures in the foreground are equally distant from the center, but the Child being on the right, the downward thrust is emphasized on the left by the position of the arm of the kneeling figure on that side, and the sword arm of St. George. The central point is frequently marked by a conspicuous object, as in this instance, the vase of flowers which not only attracts attention to the chief point of interest, but also makes the location of the fulcrum of the balance clearer to the observer. In Botticelli's Madonna and Saints (Fig. 44), the child is on the right and St. John stands farther from the center, which is marked by objects in the foreground, than does the other Saint. There is also here the downward thrust of the staff of St. John. In the Madonna, Child and Angels, by a pupil of Botticelli (Fig. 15), the more obvious method is employed of placing the Child and three Angels on the left, and four Angels and a book on the right. In Andrea del Sarto's Madonna of the Harpies (Fig. 20), there are fewer figures and any mistake in balance would be more surely felt. The Child is very much to the left, but the balance is well sustained by the tense arm of the Madonna, and the greater interest in the Saint to the right, who turns his full face toward the spectators. It must be remembered also that in all these pictures the color plays an important part. In the Holy Family, by a pupil of Botticelli (Fig. 16), the Child and two Angels are placed on the left and only one Angel on the right, but the latter figure is larger, and there is in addition the robe of the Madonna and the heavy balustrade. It is doubtful, however, whether these factors well balance the four faces to the left, especially as the interest is so much greater on that side. There is here a conflict of forces which is in very sharp contrast to Raphael's Granduca Madonna (Fig. 18), where the Madonna's head is to the left at about the golden section, and the Child to the right, its weight being further balanced by the mass of color in the Madonna's gown. Although a single figure is seldom placed in the center of the picture we find this done in the David of Pollaiuolo (Fig. 24). He is, however, not symmetrically posed, for one foot is behind the other, and one arm bent while the other arm is almost straight. In the San Sebastian, ascribed to Pollaiuolo (Fig. 32), the post is to the right, and balances the figure whose greater bulk is to the left of the central line. How much more artistic this is than it would be if the post and figure were grouped in the center. In the Portrait of a Young Woman by the artist called Amico di Sandro (Fig. 28), the figure is also placed pleasingly off center to the left. The perpendicular axis through the body is almost exactly at the golden section and the balance is secured by the white mass on the right, and the suggestion of vista through the open door. This latter factor, however, is not very strong since there are no objects within the vista to effect an adjustment in the third dimension such as may be obtained in the Madonna and Child of the Florentine School, XV Century (Fig. 14). Here the Child, a very large and robust infant, is placed very much to one side of the center. Even the Madonna's head is inclined in that direction, but the vista on the right beyond the column completely holds the balance. The effect of the vista is also clearly seen in the left side of Bordone's Doge and Fisherman (Fig. 48), where it has to counterbalance the effect produced by the interest and relatively greater weight of the scene on the right, and does so very successfully. In Ghirlandaio's Adoration (Fig. 64), there is a very considerable sweep back into the depth of the picture, and its effect is added to the weight of the main figures in the foreground to balance the hill and the interesting procession of small figures on the left; yet it is a question whether this vista is not so strong as to unbalance the picture. It certainly seems to do so in the right hand picture of the Two Portraits in Flemish Costume after the manner of Van der Goes (Fig. 33), where it should balance the large book and the head of the woman, but although the book would from its size alone suggest great weight, this effect is counteracted by the lack of strain in the hands and arms, as previously described, so that the picture seems to be pulled toward the right.

An interesting balance is seen in del Sarto's Annunciation (Fig. 49), where the fulcrum is marked by the man in the central background, and the combined weight of the large upright figure of the Virgin and the not too detailed architectural mass is offset by the three closely grouped figures of the

Angels. The subtle balance achieved by del Sarto
is one of the many factors which lend charm to his
pictures. Another example is his Madonna of the
Sack (Fig. 54), where the Madonna and Child are
placed close to the center, forming a heavy mass,
which is balanced by the figure of Joseph and a
heavy sack placed nearer the edge. Bartolommeo, in his Deposition (Fig. 55), has placed the
weight of three figures on the left and has successfully counterbalanced it by the violent and almost
unpleasant downward thrust of the bent figure on
the right. It is due alone to the exceedingly strong
empathic response aroused by this figure that the
proper distribution of weight is accomplished.
Still greater development in the distribution of
masses is seen in da Vinci's St. Ann, Virgin and
Child (Fig. 56), where a very detailed analysis of
lines and color is necessary to understand the perfect equilibrium attained. The head of St. Ann,
the most prominent of the three faces, is placed at
the golden section, and the light and shade and
direction of lines are masterfully distributed in relation to it. With equal skill and ingenuity, Raphael has obtained a balance about his central
point of interest in both his Disputa (Fig. 39), and
Heliodorus (Fig. 66). What in the hands of a less
talented artist would have been a tiresome arrangement has been made interesting for all time
by the carefully thought out variation in the direction of the movements and the distribution of the
color values. This is especially seen in the Helio-

dorus where the vigorous action of the few figures on the right is balanced by the greater crowd on the left. A still more remarkable arrangement is that in Michael Angelo's Creation of Man (Fig. 57) where the solitary figure of Adam, in spite of his reclining with full weight on the extreme left, could not balance the great mass of figures on the right if an impression of lightness were not given to the latter by its movement toward the center, and by its self-buoyancy as it floats in mid-air.

In contrast to the perfection of these compositions is Ghirlandaio's Birth of the Virgin (Fig. 60), where, notwithstanding the "weight" given by the interest in the scene on the right, the great mass of the five upright figures, the column, the stairs, and the interesting little scene of the visitation tip the picture to the left. Still greater weight must have been given to this left side by those who were acquainted with the personages portrayed. An agreeable change is at once noticed if one covers the stairs at the extreme right; the composition becomes pleasantly restful.

Thus far, we have been describing horizontal balance. Three degrees of success in perpendicular stability are exemplified: In Botticelli's Coronation (Fig. 36), in Raphael's Coronation (Fig. 37), and in his Madonna of Foligno (Fig. 38). Botticelli has placed too much weight in the upper half, and we feel the unpleasant downward thrust. In the first mentioned picture of Raphael's, there is a more equal distribution of mass and the upper figures are made light by the support of the floating clouds; but he is still more successful in the Foligno, where the center of gravity is still lower in the picture.

CHAPTER XI

THE ART IMPULSE

§ 1. Methods of Investigation

THERE are two methods of approach to the investigation of the origin and development of the art impulse, both of which have been profitable in that they are supplementary to each other. The one is a study of the development of the impulse in the individual, especially during the early years; the other, that of its manifestation in primitive peoples. Child study and anthropological investigations are of equal importance as sources of information relative to the nature of the activity, and probably also in regard to the general development of æsthetic expression. In so far as the forms of the manifestation of this activity are concerned, however, more weight must be attached to the results obtained from anthropological inquiries, than to those from investigations among children of cultured races, since such children are surrounded from birth with highly developed art forms. Nevertheless, conjectures from the productions of primitive peoples, as well as from those of children, must be made with great caution. As Professor Yrjoe Hirn has stated, "In almost every case where the ornaments of a tribe have been closely examined, it has appeared that what to us seems a

mere embellishment is for the natives in question,
full of practical, non-æsthetic significance. Carv-
ings on weapons and implements, tattooings,
woven and plaited patterns, all of which the un-
critical observer is apt to take for purely artistic
compositions, are now explained as religious symbols, owners' marks, or ideograms. . . . Wherever ethnologists have the opportunity of gaining
some insight into the inner life of a savage tribe,
they are surprised at the religious or magical significance which lies concealed behind the most
apparently trivial of amusements. And it is to be
remarked that they have learned to appreciate
this esoteric meaning, not by a closer study of the
manifestations themselves, but through information acquired by intercourse with the natives." [1]
It is especially important to have this in mind when
we come to a discussion of the various motives
underlying the art forms. Similarly in regard to
the productions of children, we must not too hastily
presume a desire for artistic activity. If the drawings of young children are examined, it will be observed that they almost invariably express more
than the children see. That is, they represent not
what the child perceives but what he knows the
object to be. Horses are depicted with the four
legs in a row, carts with the four wheels in full outline. Faces, even in profile, will have both eyes
represented. These mistakes in drawing are due
to the fact that the dominant motive is to com-

[1] *The Origins of Art*, pp. 10–11.

municate information, namely, that the horse has
four legs, the cart four wheels, the man two eyes,
etc. A certain child, when asked to draw a school-
house, outlined the façade of the building with a
door and many windows, and placed on one side of
the paper beside the house, rows of children, desks,
chairs and series of the letters of the alphabet,
which objects, according to the child's own account,
were included to tell what happened at school. It
is not always possible to tell merely from the inspection of the drawing what was the underlying
motive for the production. It is likewise frequently difficult to determine from such evidence
at exactly what period the development of the art
impulse occurs. In making a distinction of motives,
therefore, and in ascertaining the sequence in the
development of artistic expression, more can be
gained from the psychological analysis of the human activities than merely from a study of art
forms, although the latter is at times very helpful.

§ 2. CRITICISM OF THEORIES OF THE ART IMPULSE

With this introduction, we may proceed to the
criticism of some of the theories concerning the
nature of the art impulse and thus to a theory
consistent with the views of the æsthetic attitude
previously stated. According to Dr. Marshall,
"The 'Art Impulse' is a blind impulse which leads
men to *create* with little or no notion of the end they
have in view. That this art impulse in one form or
another is a common heritage of the members of

our race is, I think, true without doubt." [1] Dr.
Marshall states further: "Nor can we with Kant
and Schiller hold that the 'art impulse' is especially
connected with the 'play impulse' through lack of
end, if I am right that an end for art work is discernible in *attraction through the pleasing of others.*" [2]
The latter part of the statement contains the essence of Dr. Marshall's real view. The impulse
is not blind in so far as the true motive of art is a
desire to attract by pleasing. We have already
criticised this hedonistic æsthetics in connection
with Grant Allen's views, on the ground that we
are given no means of differentiating various forms
of pleasure. It was previously shown (page 35)
that Dr. Marshall agrees with this criticism. He
would undoubtedly be the last to insist that every
form of pleasurable attraction is æsthetic, or even
that an attraction in itself was an essential characteristic or motive in æsthetic creation.

Professor Mark J. Baldwin, although stressing the
importance in art production as well as in play, of
attraction which, according to his theory, involves
the self-exhibition impulse, is aware of the danger
of such a generalization, for he states that "the
theory . . . which identifies the art impulse with
the self-exhibiting impulse, is consistently evolu-
tionary; but it has failed to find, in my view, that
the self-exhibiting impulses have either the important function or the degree of exercise which the

[1] *Pain, Pleasure and Æsthetics*, pp. 100–101.
[2] *Ibid.*, p. 104.

derivation of the art-impulse from them would demand." [1] Nevertheless, psychology has shown that the self-exhibiting factor is an important motive in all human pursuits. Whether it is art, public speaking, teaching, politics, or business, man is concerned to a greater or less degree with the exhibition of his ego.

Almost all descriptions of the art impulse have emphasized its non-practical aspect and the fact that there does not appear to be any aim beyond the immediate activity itself. This seeming characteristic has led many authors to identify the art impulse with play. Further inquiry has shown that art has a practical value and aim, but the same arguments may be used in the case of play, so that there is still the possibility of an identification between the two impulses or instincts, as they are frequently termed.

§ 3. THE NATURE OF THE PLAY IMPULSE

Among the classical theories of play, those of Schiller and Spencer have figured most prominently. Both authors based their theories on the excess or superabundance of energy. The passage in which Schiller expresses his views most clearly is the following: "No doubt nature has given more than is necessary to unreasoning beings; she has caused a gleam of freedom to shine even in the darkness of animal life. When the lion is not tormented

[1] *Social and Ethical Interpretations in Mental Development,* 3d edition, p. 161.

by hunger, and when no wild beast challenges him to fight, his unemployed energy creates an object for himself; full of ardour, he fills the re-echoing desert with his terrible roars, and his exuberant force rejoices in itself, showing itself without an object. The insect flits about rejoicing in life in the sunlight, and it is certainly not the cry of want that makes itself heard in the melodious song of the bird; there is undeniably freedom in these movements, though it is not emancipation from want in general, but from a determinative external necessity.

"The animal *works*, when a privation is the motor [incitement] of its activity, and it *plays* when the plenitude of force is this motor [incitement], when an exuberant life is excited to action. Even in inanimate nature a luxury of strength and a latitude of determination are shown, which in this material sense might be styled play." [1]

In a similar manner Spencer writes: "Inferior kinds of animals have in common the trait, that all their forces are expended in fulfilling functions essential to the maintenance of life. They are unceasingly occupied in searching for food, in escaping from enemies, in forming places of shelter, and in making preparations for progeny. But as we ascend to animals of high types, having faculties more efficient and more numerous, we begin to

---

[1] *Essays, Æsthetical and Philosophical* (Bohn's Libraries), Letter XXVII, pp. 112–113. This has been quoted by Professor Groos in *The Play of Animals*, p. 2.

find that time and strength are not wholly absorbed in providing for immediate needs. Better nutrition, gained by superiority, occasionally yields a surplus of vigour. The appetites being satisfied, there is no craving which directs the overflowing energies to the pursuit of more prey, or to the satisfaction of some pressing want." He goes on to explain that when the nerve centers are for a long time unused, since repair goes on day and night the centers are brought into a state of more than ordinary instability. . . . Hence, play of all kinds—hence this tendency to superfluous and useless exercise of faculties that have been quiescent." [1] For Schiller *"physical play* or the *free movement* which is itself its own end and means" is a link in the transition from *"physical seriousness* to æsthetical play" which has no special aim.[2] And similarly for Spencer, "The higher but less essential powers, as well as the lower but more essential powers, thus come to have activities that are carried on for the sake of the immediate gratification derived, without reference to ulterior benefits; and to such higher powers, æsthetic products yield these substituted activities, as games yield them to various lower powers." [3]

The criticism that was previously made of the assumed independence of æsthetic pleasure from life-serving functions applies equally well to Spen-

[1] *Principles of Psychology*, vol. II, part 2, Appleton, 1900, pp. 628–630.
[2] *Essays Æsthetical and Philosophical*, p. 113.
[3] *Op. cit.*, p. 632.

cer's theory which makes freedom from "immediate needs" and from "reference to ulterior benefits" a characteristic of the art impulse. In regard to play, which seems to be identified with the art impulse, Schiller's and Spencer's ideas of stored-up or superabundant energies have no positive physiological facts to back them. Spencer is cautious when he speaks of it as "A state of more than ordinary instability—a state of excessive readiness to decompose and discharge," [1] but he does not account for the numerous instances of play where the child or primitive man not only continues but even initiates frolic when he is too fatigued to work, and where he drops from exhaustion before he can be induced to stop. Who has not, as a child, felt a sudden realization of extreme weariness when he has been called from his play to perform some useful chore? Experience also contradicts the theory that motor energies which have been denied an outlet in the reactions of the routine work of the day find such expression in games. It does not matter how active the child has been— and there are few muscles that an active child does not use—seldom will he refuse to join in a game, and frequently the more tired he is, the more restless and desirous of doing something he becomes. [2]

There has been added to the surplus energy the-

[1] *Op. cit.*, p. 629.

[2] Professor Groos gives a number of examples from the play of man and animals such as the play of dogs after they seem entirely exhausted, *The Play of Animals*, pp. 19-22. See also McDougall, *Social Psychology*, pp. 107-108.

ory that of the desire for recreation, but as Professor Groos has pointed out this is applicable to only a limited sphere.[1]   Indeed, it is doubtful if this is ever the sole motive.   Such theories as the above, then, though extremely suggestive and in some of their aspects founded upon facts, are inadequate to explain the general characteristics underlying the play activity.   What has been said of the surplus energy theory applies equally to theories based upon the assumption of a "normal amount of activity in any portion or the whole of the organism." [2]

Professor Groos, after showing the inadequacy of the energy theory, formulates one derived from his extensive investigations of the play of man and animals, and based upon the primitive development of instincts and the law of natural selection. "The play of young animals has its origin in the fact that certain very important instincts appear at a time when the animal does not seriously need them. . . . The utility of play is incalculable. The utility consists in the practice and exercise it affords for some of the more important duties of life." [3]   And further, "Animals cannot be said to play because they are young and frolicsome, but rather they have a period of youth in order to play." [4]   There are many objections to this theory,

[1] *Op. cit.*, p. 17.

[2] Grant Allen, *Psychological Æsthetics*, p. 22. Other theories such as the recapitulation theory and the atavistic theory are highly speculative.

[3] *Op. cit.*, pp. 75–76.

[4] *Ibid.*, p. 75.

important among which are that a teleological principle is invoked, and the fact that even if the instincts enumerated are admitted, we have gained very little knowledge of the nature of the activity. On the other hand, the theory has the advantage, shared with most of those of modern times, of emphasizing the biological significance of play.

Professor McDougall [1] criticises Professor Groos's theory on the ground that many of the instincts do not appear in their true form in play—dogs do not actually bite one another, although they are sufficiently developed to do so—and also because it cannot explain many of the plays of children which are not directly due to instincts. Professor McDougall, in fact, denies that play can be ascribed to an instinct; rather, it is a tendency and "must be reckoned among native tendencies of the mind of high social value." [2] He lays great stress upon the motives underlying play, especially those of getting the better of, emulating, and excelling others. Professor McDougall's criticisms are well founded and his positive statements are cautious and suggestive, and although not developed sufficiently to give an entirely satisfactory description, mark a decided advance.

A recent theory based upon instincts, is that of Norsworthy and Whitley, who state that "so-called play resolves into the functioning of gradually ripening instincts evoked by situations not stamped

[1] *Social Psychology*, pp. 108 *et seq.*
[2] *Ibid.*, p. 107.

with the economic need which would lead us to call the activity work." [1]   Influenced by the suggestions of Professor Thorndike,[2] they assert that in a more primitive environment where the needs are more insistent, what is called "play" would be termed "work." What has previously been said concerning instincts applies equally here. In addition, it is a question among scientists (granted that there are such instincts), whether there is this "gradual ripening," upon which they have based their deductions. The description, however, has the advantage of not relying upon innate tendencies, but placing great importance upon the influence of the environment. The theory of Miss Appleton [3] to which they refer, and which makes play dependent upon the structure of the body, attempts to explain the various forms of play which develop, according to the requirements of the organism, rather than to investigate the general characteristics.

For our purpose, it seems more advantageous instead of invoking mysterious instincts and impulses as explanation both of play and art, to attempt a brief description of the facts in the development of play in the child, and to compare this with what we know of artistic creation. According to the generally accepted principle in psychology, every stimulation of the organism must have a

---

[1] *Psychology and Childhood*, p. 210.

[2] *Original Nature of Man*, p. 146.

[3] *A Comparative Study of the Activities of Adult Savages, and Civilized Children.*

motor outlet. In the early stages of life, shortly before and after birth, these movements, due to touch and pressure from without and within, to stimulations of light and sound, etc., seem to be almost entirely incoördinated and random. This much can be said, however, that whenever these movements are blocked by some external force, there is a persistence of the movement which has a tendency to overcome the obstacle. The repetition of movement is due to the fact that the sensation caused by the resisting object discharges through the motor path of least resistance, and that is the one that has just been used. Many believe that the unimpeded activity is pleasant, and the blocked movement unpleasant.

At any rate, various muscular coördinations, developed through chance, are found by the individual useful in his later adaptation to his environment. These coördinations of necessity become increasingly complex in nature, so that the child constantly finds itself in situations which call for a nicer adaptation and adjustment than it has at its command. It therefore "makes" an environment for itself, commensurate with its abilities. We are accustomed to speak of such activities as play. What the form will be depends upon conditions. The children of the most primitive peoples have had to be content with the simplest products of the imagination. The child of to-day has many forms of play provided for it. There is also the added fact that the range for imitation has become in-

creasingly great. Imitation itself can be explained
as a natural effect of the surroundings, as can also
the various important motives, such as rivalry,
emulation, etc. According to this description, it
is not an instinct of play that develops certain situations, but the interaction of organism and environment that develops a certain activity which has
been termed "play."

That play results from this conflict of the desire
early developed by the lessons of experience to
adapt ourselves to the many situations of life, and
to the lack of the ability to do so, is seen especially
in the case of the delicate child who, instead of
playing with boisterous and vigorous companions,
withdraws to a world of its own imagination, peo-
pled with fanciful playmates who speak a language
probably only partly intelligible to itself. Such a
world becomes so real to it that it is only from
another's point of view that the activity is called
play. For the child the playmates exist, and so
vividly are they present that often there is a howl
of real anguish if a "grown-up" inadvertently sits
upon a chair already occupied by one of its imaginary companions.

§ 4. The Social Factor in the Art Impulse

In all forms of play there is so close a resemblance
to artistic creation that it is small wonder that the
two have been identified. At first thought, the
children's play of "Mother and Father," or of "Indians," since all the characteristics of dramatic

construction are present, seems to show the dawn of æsthetic production, but that is a judgment based alone upon the form of expression. One essential feature is absent, and that is the social factor, the desire to communicate the experience to others. If we add this characteristic to play, we have the æsthetic. A child may dress as an Indian and be content to play by itself for hours at a time, but at some period it will demand an audience to watch it perform, and it will expect to share its pleasure with the onlookers. This may come very early in a child's life, but whenever it does come it marks a new epoch in its series of experiences. This social element is never essential for play. Often the pleasure is greater without companions, but even when the child does demand mates, they are there as part of the game, as are also the sofas and chairs, to be ordered about and handled, and not purely as playfellows nor yet as spectators. Indeed there is a very marked absence of the social quality in the play of children. How rarely, for example, do we see any expression of sympathy among them. If one, for some reason, begins to cry, the others continue their sport so utterly oblivious of their companion's sorrow, that for the adult onlooker, the scene is ludicrous.

The social factor in art has frequently been mentioned [1] although it has not always been so specific-

---

[1] For Professor Baldwin self-exhibition is a social factor in art, since there is present the desire for approval in an audience. According to his statement "The social judgment, which a work of art has to sustain, finds its

ally emphasized as a distinguishing feature of the activity, as has been done by Guyau, who states that, "the artistic emotion is then essentially social. Its result is to enlarge the individual's life in causing it to merge into a larger and more universal life. The highest aim of art is to produce an æsthetic emotion of a social nature." [1] Professor Hirn has also observed the social side: "In order to understand the art impulse as a tendency to æsthetic production, we must bring it into connection with some function, from the nature of which the specifically artistic qualities may be derived. Such a function is to be found, we believe, in the activities of emotional expression." [2] Further on he adds: "The work of art presents itself as the most effective means by which the individual is enabled to convey to wider and wider circles of sympathizers an emotional state similar to that by which

correlative impulse in the self-exhibition of the producer." (*Social and Ethical Interpretations in Mental Developments*, p. 150.) There is, however, more than this wish for approval or social support which, indeed, is present in many non-æsthetic impulses, namely, the desire to have others share our pleasure through "participation" in our æsthetic production.

Although Dr. Ernst Grosse made absence of purpose in art an essential difference between art and play he nevertheless recognized the social function of art, for he has written: "The artist labors not only for himself but for others; and although one cannot say that the only incentive to artistic creation is a desire to impress other people, yet the forms and development of art are determined essentially through the consideration of a public,—not so much as it exists but as it is idealized by the artist. In fact a work of art presupposes a public, just as much as it does an artist." (*Die Anfänge der Kunst*, p. 47.)

[1] *L'art au point de vue sociologique*, p. 21.
[2] *The Origins of Art*, p. 29.

he is himself dominated." [1] In short, there are other means of communicating ideas, but art is the only form in which the emotional states are communicated for their own sake. That ideas are communicated by art is, of course, true, but they are presented in such a form that others are able to have the same pleasure as recipients of the ideas that we have had in their conception. They are thus given the opportunity to participate in our æsthetic life. It is undoubtedly this characteristic of art to which Guyau refers when he speaks of an enlargement of the individual life. Just as there are other modes of communicating ideas, so there are other ways of communicating emotion, but in such non-æsthetic situations it is not that we desire another to participate in our affective life through æsthetic empathy, but rather to respond with a corresponding emotion as love, or to react with what might be termed a complementary response, as when one in anger shakes a fist at one's enemy. In this latter situation, it is not the emotion of anger but that of fear, with its corresponding reaction, that we are desirous of arousing. There is an effect in this instance beyond the mere shaking of the fist. How disconcerting it would be under such circumstances to obtain an æsthetic response, such as would be indicated by the enemy remarking, "What a delightful pose."

It is often stated that artistic work is not produced with the thought of an audience, and the

[1] *The origin of Art*, p. 85.

objection to the above theory will be made that many artists have no idea of a public when they are creating. Indeed, we frequently hear the statement from artists, perhaps in defensory reaction to criticism, that they do not care what people think; that further it is a matter of complete indifference whether any one sees the picture or not. It is truly a lowering of the standard of art to create merely for the sake of pleasing the public, especially when we do not approve of its standards. Every true artist will rebel against the idea of "catering" to anyone, but is there not somewhere in the corner of the artist's mind the desire for some audience? If the human beings with whom he is immediately surrounded are not deemed by him sufficiently developed æsthetically and therefore worthy of the privilege of viewing his production, then does he not create a sympathetic audience out of his imagination, an ideal construction which meets his highest standard of appreciation? If we should say to an artist who had retired from the world with the products of his artistic creation that we knew a man who was capable of understanding his work, and who would be in sympathy with it, would not his eyes glow with pleasure, and if he had not grown too skeptical from bitter disappointment, would he not insist upon meeting the man? In all situations in life, we seek sympathy and understanding, but the artist finds it essential and creates such an audience in imagination if it is not given to him in reality. The poor, neglected poet who has given up hope of being heard, still composes to some one, to the angels if you will. Even Robinson Crusoe on his seemingly deserted island, without an expectation of seeing a human being, if in a moment of artistic fervor, he had sketched upon the sand, would have done so with the social idea somewhere present in his consciousness, and surely one of the satisfactions of Friday's appearance upon the scene would have been the response that Crusoe would have obtained regarding his sketch.

Another distinction that has rightly been made between play and art, is that the former is evanescent while the latter has the quality of permanence. This demand for permanence is included in the desire for communication, in that we desire the form to be lasting in order to have as large an audience as possible. It is not necessary for an object to have this quality of permanence in order to be considered beautiful. The medium employed may be a matter of chance and does not concern us here. The psychology of the situation does, however, and certainly the artist's ideal is conspicuously one of permanence, just as it is one of social communication. It seems hardly believable that if an artist, in a less serious mood, had successfully carved a statue in ice, he would not have regretted the medium chosen. On the other hand, there would be no such feeling of loss in regard to a form of play, and here again the fundamental difference between the two activities may be seen, for it is not a matter of degree but of essential human motives. It seems safe to say that no art form would have come into existence if it were not for the hope of an audience, real or imaginary. It is only in this sense of permanency for social reasons that the beauty of a work of art may be considered as resting in the object, for the possible audience is presupposed and the beauty is thus a latent possibility.

The impulse to create works of art may then be considered not identical with, but a development from, the play impulse, through the addition of the desire for social expression and communication. In the æsthetic attitude, which is one of appreciation, there is in common with play the desire to become satisfactorily adjusted to a situation, but it is doubtful whether the social factor is necessarily present except perhaps in the æsthetic attitude toward nature where there is an element of creation as well as appreciation. Even here, however, the social factor does not seem to be as essential as it is in the creation of art.

Æsthetic appreciation must be present before there can be artistic production. Being thus prior to the creation of permanent forms of beauty its earliest manifestations must have been in the contemplation of those natural objects which offered the opportunity for the successful coördination of the organism; and these first æsthetic pleasures must have been in this smooth and harmonious adjustment which means a complete unification of the individual and his immediate world.

§ 5. Development of the Art Impulse

That this pleasure occurs very early in the development of the race, and that it appears in early childhood is safe to assume, but just when such a consciousness of beauty arises is very difficult to say, for it is impossible to judge the exact period of such mental development, either in primitive peoples or children, merely from the form of their activity. It is, for instance, fallacious to conclude that an infant has acted from an artistic impulse when it consistently chooses one color rather than another from a series of colored papers presented to it, since any one of a number of factors may condition the choice, such as the brightness of a particular color which causes it to stand out from the others and thus to attract the attention, or the association of the color with some familiar object to which the child has already become adjusted. Indeed, without further evidence, such a reaching out for a color or attention to a sound, although interesting from the point of view of child behavior, should not be included in æsthetic choices any more than the reaction of a bull to a red flag. It is only later, when the child can give more evidence, through words, of its motive, that we can be sure.

The delight in rhythmical movement for its own sake is undoubtedly the fundamental factor in the dance, music, and in poetry, if not in all forms of art, and one that appears very early. There are many productions of young children that bear the

indubitable stamp of artistic creation. Who can
doubt that the four-year old authoress of the following lines had already many times experienced
the joy of sound and rhythm until it burst into expression?

> "There is going to be the sound of bells
> And murmuring.
> This is the brook dance;
> There is going to be the sound of voices,
> And the smallest will be the brook:
> It is the song of water
> You will hear,
> A little winding song
> To dance to. . . ." [1]

The artistic sense frequently develops very rapidly
and without any deliberate influence from the
parents. At the age of nine this same child wrote:

> "Orchid Lady
> Tan-and-green orchid,
> Are you a little lady
> Holding up your skirts
> Above wet grass?
> Do you wear a feather
> Where that white is showing?
> Is there any color
> Shut inside your heart?
> I could be an orchid,
> I could be a lady,
> I could wear a feather,
> I could step like you:

[1] From a collection of verse by Hilda Conkling entitled *Poems by a Little Girl*.

> There is just the difference
> Of your way of bowing,
> And your tilted bonnet
> And your satin shoe!" [1]

There are several other human impulses which have been supposed to underlie that of art, such as the sex instinct, the instinct of combat, and the desire to prepare for future activities, which includes the idea of usefulness. These various phases of human activity, however, merely present the opportunity for the development, and cannot be considered in the same relation to the art impulse as is play.[2]

Sex attraction has seemed to a number of writers a very important motive for the art impulse, and Darwin's description of the attraction among animals might seem to lend weight to this, since among animals at least one of the sexes is frequently beautifully colored, especially in the mating season. That such colors may attract the opposite sex is quite possible, but it has no point to speak of the æsthetic value of such factors. That they often seem beautiful to us is true, but whether it means anything more to the animal than the attraction of attention by intense stimuli, can no more be answered than in the case of the infant. If the æsthetic quality is invoked, then the animal must have already had

---

[1] Unpublished poem by Hilda Conkling.

[2] For a description of the imagination of children in play and art, of the earliest art forms in children and primitive people and of the genetic development of the dance, music, poetry, etc., see Wilhelm Wundt, *Völkerpsychologie*, vol. 2, part 1.

the æsthetic sense developed before it could be attracted, and it would thus be, so far as appreciation is concerned, quite independent of any sexual instinct. As a matter of fact, modern investigations have shown that the colors of animals serve a very different purpose, namely, that of protection, and although that does not exclude the possibility of a second form of usefulness, it throws doubt upon it. Even the most brilliant colors, such as the beautiful combinations in the peacock's tail have been shown by Mr. Abbott Thayer to be protective coloring. When the animal sits in the tree, the feathers blend with the bright leaves, forming a patch of sunlight, which attracts the eye away from the body of the bird. Even the marvelously intense red of the flamingo blends with the sunrise and sunset colors of the sky, protecting the bird at the time it is most likely, on account of its feeding habits, to be seen on the horizon.[1]

The savage may have obtained his or her ideas of self-decoration from the animal and have used it for sex attraction, even without any idea of beauty. Colors that one's mate has worn may later become pleasant by association without having any æsthetic value in themselves. The æsthetic feeling is here offered an opportunity for

[1] See *Concealing Coloration in the Animal Kingdom* by Gerald H. Thayer, in which is described the theory by Abbott Handerson Thayer.

For a criticism of the various theories on the origin of music, including a refutation of Darwin's hypothesis concerning the music of animals and its bearing on sex attraction see Carl Stumpf, *Anfänge der Musik*, pp. 7–61, and Richard Wallaschek, *Primitive Music*, Chapter IX.

development, but certainly it cannot be said to be more than superficially related to the sexual desire, nor can it be admitted that the æsthetically pleasing is merely a matter of association.

There is no doubt, on the other hand, that some of the forms of the dance have originated for sexual purposes. In certain tribes, for example, there is a dance performed by the virgins before the older women for the instruction of the former in sexual matters. Such a dance may appear to be graceful and will then survive long after the rite has lost its original meaning for the æsthetic pleasure it affords. In the Orient many of the dances are merely for the arousal of passions, and there is no pretense at maintaining an æsthetic attitude. The sex impulse is certainly the most important for life, and probably has afforded the most opportunities for developing a particular form of beauty, but it cannot be considered the only incentive, nor should it be over-emphasized. Fabre, for example, has intimated that the Tarantella probably originated from the custom of dancing wildly when bitten by the tarantula in order to eliminate the poison through the skin, and many other forms of dance have had their origin in the arousal of the religious emotion or the fighting spirit, and have survived through custom and tradition.[1]

---

[1] The savage has had to imagine an environment suitable for its purpose, just as the child does. Many dances probably had their origin in the necessity to prepare for combat, even though they may have been continued for other reasons and as Wallaschek has written: " if daily life at times does not

Many conventional forms have not much semblance to beauty, although since they resemble art forms and have no longer a purpose, they are looked upon as such. Examples may be found in styles in clothing, such as the buttons on a man's sleeve, or the slit in the back of the coat, formerly for the sword. The retention of such forms is certainly not dictated by a sense of beauty. Even the headgear of the primitive fighters, such as the feathers of the Indian, or the mammoth headpieces of more modern fighters, although they may now seem æsthetically pleasing to us, were used to frighten the enemy. Many of the forms we find in art, and this is especially true of primitive art, were originally due to practical considerations. The round hut was the shape best suited for construction out of supple boughs, since they could be easily bent over, their two ends being fastened to the ground. In the Orient, many of the rooms are long and very narrow, because sufficiently long timber could not be obtained to sustain a wide ceiling, and not because such a shape was considered pleasing, although doubtless one accustomed from childhood to such proportions, might think any other form queer. Many of the forms of vases and cooking utensils were chosen for their adaptation to their purpose, and the markings of the tools had frequently a specific use other than that of beauty. We must also be careful in assuming the

offer any occasion for war the latter must be invented, and the one who possesses this power of invention is in fact the 'artist,'" *op. cit.*, p. 273.

origin of so-called personal adornment to be an artistic impulse. For instance, the faces of the del Fuego Indian women are frequently decorated with stripes of paint, but in the case of widows this is done in order to inform the world of the manner of death of the late husband, a wavy line being death by drowning, a jagged line being death through a fall or by lightning, etc. Even the wearing of clothing by women of many tribes was not for adornment or even through the sense of modesty, but as a means of protection against evil spirits. There are also those forms which were used purely for the communication of ideas, such as hieroglyphics and picture writing, and also other designs such as the totem, obelisk, etc., which are symbolical.

Thus we see the many possible motives that underlie what may seem to be the creative artistic impulse, but which merely offer the suggestion for the direction which this impulse may take when it appears. We shall then find that most of these forms have been modified along the lines of beauty, away from their original purpose. The lines will have been made more graceful, the rhythm more perfect, the balance more pleasing, and the unity more complete. It seems safe to say that unless the forms offer such possibility of modification in the direction of the æsthetically pleasing, that is so that the organism can readily adapt itself to them, the most conservative race will not retain them for all time through mere convention. Even such long established but useless and unattractive forms as are found in the modern dress will gradually vanish, never to appear again.

Finally there is the interesting fact that we find not merely the general artistic sense and the desire to create, but even very similar forms of artistic expression early in the race's history and among primitive peoples and children. It is true that if we find similar forms in two races geographically widely separated, it is frequently because these races have a common origin or have had means of communication with each other. This is the principle that is the most stimulating for anthropological and ethnological research and by which such investigations must be primarily guided, but most are agreed that this principle is not everywhere valid. Often surprising similarity in art forms is found between races that could hardly have had a common origin or means of communication, such as the resemblance of certain music of the del Fuego Indians at the southern tip of South America with that of the Indians of New Mexico. Underlying the resemblance is the psychological fact that rhythm is the most fundamental of reactions. Indeed very striking resemblances in rhythmical expressions are found in practically all peoples. Another example of the similarity of art forms out of the hundreds that might be mentioned is that of the "Stave-kirke" of Norway, which resembles certain architectural designs of the Chinese. Perhaps the best known design is that of the swastika which is found in almost every race. If we admit certain common characteristics of the human organism, and similar features existing in different environments, the explanation of such resemblances is very evident. The common art forms are merely the result of the general modes of action which are bound to be developed in the course of adaptation of an organism like ours to the natural forces of a planet like the earth.[1] The fact that this similarity of expression has been so frequently found, strengthens the hope of eventually obtaining many valid æsthetic laws for the human race.

[1] Anthropologists refer to this cause of the origin of similar art forms as one of "psychic unity." Such a theory, in some respects, resembles the hypothesis of "monotypical evolution," namely, that all races have a common course of development.

CHAPTER XII

CONCLUSION

THIS last chapter is a brief summary of the most important facts of the book, together with an indication of their interrelation and their wider application to the problems of human happiness.

Whenever we are able to adjust ourselves successfully to a situation, so that our responses are unified into a well-integrated or organized form of action, we call that situation beautiful, and the accompanying feeling one of æsthetic pleasure. Whenever the situation is such that unified adjustment is impossible the object seems ugly and the feeling is one of æsthetic pain. If the human organism were perfectly adjusted to all the varying conditions of its environment the world would appear entirely beautiful and there would be no more pleasure in beauty than there would be in the sunlight if it were constantly present. The amount of pleasure in a given situation depends, in part, upon the degree of difficulty in the attainment of the adjustment. A study of the genetic aspect of beauty has shown that an adjustment may be too easy as well as too difficult to be entirely pleasant. For the maximum amount of pleasure the required adjustment should be commensurate with the capacity of the organism at the time. Together with this realization of successful adjustment there is a certain feeling of efficiency which is an added inspiration for further action.

Although the adjustments which we make are those of our organism they are projected into the object we are observing. In this way they seem to be a part or characteristic of the object. For example the grace of a serpentine line seems to be a characteristic of that line even though we may know that our pleasure is the immediate result of the ease of our adjustment to the curve. Strictly, however, neither grace nor any other form of beauty is in the object or in the organism. Beauty is a specific relation of the two, for whether a particular adjustment will be a well-organized one, whether indeed it can be carried out at all, depends upon both the organism and the object to which it responds.

Not every relation to our environment has the possibility of arousing in us an æsthetic pleasure. The response is to beauty only when the conditions are such that the adjustment itself is the source of pleasure. The necessary conditions for æsthetic pleasure are those which have been described as fundamental to the æsthetic attitude, namely, when the total situation is so constituted that we are guided in our contemplation only by those clues which are given directly by the object of beauty, or those suggestions which are in harmony with it. In principle such an attitude can be assumed toward any object from fountain pens to Paradise

Lost. Whether or not a particular object will call forth such an attitude, however, depends upon the state of mind of the individual at the time.

Our æsthetic pleasure in the successful adjustment to the ordinary things of daily life is more common than is perhaps realized. Equally frequent is the pain caused by our inability to find a satisfactory outlet for those responses which are the expression of our impulses and desires. The great function of art is to provide this outlet. When we are beset with perplexities of life which are beyond our power to solve, and our imagination is inadequate to create for ourselves a desirable situation, we turn to the artist who gives us all that he has and who asks from us little more in return than that we shall be an echo of his thoughts and pleasures. It is not surprising, then, that the artist is so often allowed a social freedom denied to others, for his joy is the joy in creating and in the generous sharing of his treasures with others.

In the many and varied forms of art each individual can find his particular refuge. The strong and the weak, the rich and the poor, the prude and the libertine, the prince and the peasant, can one and all select that form of art in which they can best realize a harmonious adjustment of the conflicting impulses which tend to torture and distort the soul. Each can find comfort according to his nature, whether it is in jazz or symphony, melodrama or classic tragedy, folk song or polyphonic prose.

So long as human personalities differ, just so long will there be sorts and degrees of beauty. So long as the human race is stirred by conflicts just so long will art itself endure. It is one of the most valuable possessions of the race, and the only one which may be enjoyed without thought of recompense. Art demands but one thing, that we remain loyal to its beauty.

INDEX

Adaptation, necessity for a new and successful, 123, 237ff.

Adjustment of the organism: to the environment, 13; in unification, 166ff.; in perception of proportion, 234; in play, 262; harmonious, 268; importance in æsthetics, 278

Æsthetic attitude, see Attitude

Æsthetics: function of, 13; definition of, 28ff.; scientific treatment of, 29ff.; rules in, 32f.; object of, 41ff.

Albertinelli, 197, 232

Allen, Grant, 19, 37, 253, 258

Amico di Sandro, 154, 245

Angelico, Fra, 152, 198

Angelo, Michael, 136, 147, 153, 198, 199, 248

Angier, R. P., 216, 226, 229

Anstruther-Thompson, C., 114, 119, 219, 220

Anthropological investigations of the art impulse, 250f., 276f.

Antinomy of distance, 72

Appleton, L. E., 260

Appreciation of beauty, 3ff.

Appreciator, relation of, to the object of beauty, 16ff.; 24ff.

Aquinas, Thomas, 47

Architecture: æsthetic attitude in, 86f.; empathy in, 131ff.; binding effect of, in pictures, 196ff.; golden section in, 232; proportions in, 235f.

Aristotle, 165

Art: history of, 18f.; industrial, 81ff.; origin of, forms, 273ff.

Art impulse: creative, 23, chapter XI; development of the, 269ff.

Artist *versus* appreciator, 13

Associated ideas, 164f.

Asymmetrical balance, 206f.; preference for, 228ff.; explanation of preference for, 236ff.; illustrations of, chapter X

Attention: a unifying process, 158ff.; direction of, by lines, 190ff.; centering of, 195ff.; attraction through detailed execution in pictures, 204f.

Attitude: various attitudes toward the environment, 39ff.; æsthetic, chapter III; motor, 71; factors in preserving the æsthetic, chapter IV

Babbit, Irving, 11

Bain, Alexander, 133

Baker, G. P., 171

Balance: of motor impulses, 55ff., 212f., 216ff., 218, 229f.; in art, chapter IX; illustrations of balance in the fine arts, chapter X.

Baldwin, Mark J., 253, 263

Barker, Granville, 94

Bartolommeo, Fra, 198, 232, 247

Beauty: relation to the good and the true, 3f.; philosophical, psychological and objective aspects of, 14ff.; theories of, 44; free 45; participation in the object of, 59ff.; relation to truth, 95ff.; relation to morality, 102ff.

Belasco, David, 184

283